GCSE
Geography
for WJEC B

Revision Guide

Stuart Currie

DYNAMIC LEARNING

HODDER
EDUCATION
AN HACHETTE UK COMPANY

The Publishers would like to thank the following for permission to reproduce copyright material:

Photo credits p.17 © Still Pictures/Jorgen Schytte; p.21 © Stuart Currie; p.30 © IOM/MPW Photography Project 2007 – Lerato Maduna; p.32, p.39 © Stuart Currie; p.42 © Photolibrary/Peter Weimann; p.54, p.55 © Stuart Currie; p.57 © Colin Lancaster; p.59 © Alamy/Andrew Palmer; photo on page 68 from www.oxfam.org.uk/applications/blogs/ pressoffice/?p=5991&newsblog by Coco McCabe, 2009 is reproduced with the permission of Oxfam GB, Oxfam House, John Smith Drive, Cowley, Oxford OX4 2JY, UK www.oxfam.org.uk. Oxfam GB does not necessarily endorse any text or activities that accompany the materials; p.76 (left) © Stringer/Hulton Archive/Getty Images; p.76 (right) © Getty Images/ Goh Chai Hin/AFP; p.95 © Eric Foxley; p.96 © Stuart Currie.

Maps on inside front cover and back cover reproduced from Ordnance Survey mapping with the permission of the Controller of HMSO, © Crown copyright. All rights reserved. Licence no. 1000364700.

Text extracts p.25 adapted from http://ecotownsyoursay.direct.gov.uk/my-eco-town/what-should-it-look-like; p.26 © CPRE, Policy Statement, March 2006; p.35 © 2002 Independent News and Media. All rights reserved. You may forward this article or obtain additional permissions at the following iCopyright license record and renewal locator: http://license.icopyright.net/3.7463-28331; p.68 adapted by the Publisher from www.oxfam.org.uk/applications/ blogs/pressoffice/?p=5991&newsblog by Coco McCabe 2009 with the permission of Oxfam GB, Oxfam House, John Smith Drive, Cowley, Oxford OX4 2JY UK www.oxfam.org.uk Oxfam GB does not necessarily endorse any text or activities that accompany the materials, nor has it approved the adapted text; p.69 © Canadian Standing Senate Committee on Foreign Affairs, 8 March 2005; p.74 © BBC News Online, 29 June 2005; p.78 © Brundtland Report, 1987.

Every effort has been made to trace all copyright holders, but if any have been inadvertently overlooked the Publishers will be pleased to make the necessary arrangements at the first opportunity.

Although every effort has been made to ensure that website addresses are correct at time of going to press, Hodder Education cannot be held responsible for the content of any website mentioned in this book. It is sometimes possible to find a relocated web page by typing in the address of the home page for a website in the URL window of your browser.

Hachette UK's policy is to use papers that are natural, renewable and recyclable products and made from wood grown in sustainable forests. The logging and manufacturing processes are expected to conform to the environmental regulations of the country of origin.

Orders: please contact Bookpoint Ltd, 130 Milton Park, Abingdon, Oxon OX14 4SB. Telephone: (44) 01235 827720. Fax: (44) 01235 400454. Lines are open 9.00–5.00, Monday to Saturday, with a 24-hour message answering service. Visit our website at www.hoddereducation.co.uk

© Stuart Currie 2010
First published in 2010 by
Hodder Education,
An Hachette UK Company
338 Euston Road
London NW1 3BH

Impression number   9 8 7 6
Year   2015 2014 2013 2012

Cover photo: Women selling food at the market, Accra, Ghana © Sven Torfinn/Panos Pictures.
Illustrations by Jeff Edwards, Julian Mosedale, Tim Oliver, Oxford Illustrators, Barking Dog and DC Graphic Design Ltd.
Editorial and layout by Hart McLeod, Cambridge
Typeset in Times 11.5pt
Printed in India

A catalogue record for this title is available from the British Library

ISBN: 978 0340 987 964

Contents

Why should I use this book? 4

Theme 1

Challenges of Living in a Built Environment 16

Theme 2

People and the Natural World Interactions 36

Theme 3

People, Work and Development 54

Problem Solving

Problem Solving 80
Foundation Tier 82
Higher Tier 88
Resource Folder 95

Shehzad Mohammad

Why should I use this book?

This revision guide has been written to accompany the WJEC GCSE Geography Specification B course, to help you get the best possible result in your examinations.

There is a great deal you need to know in order to obtain a result you will be proud of in this subject. To get the best out of the examination you will need to know geography. In addition you will need to understand exactly what the examiner wants of you and be able to provide this in the examination situation.

But don't panic – that's where this guide comes in! It takes you back through all the main areas of content for your course and will also train you in how to use this information to get the best out of your exams. By the time you have finished you will know almost as much about these as your examiners do – not a bad position to be in!

So, please don't ignore the opening pages of this guide. They are the key to getting the best out of the rest of the book and, as a result, obtaining the best possible result for *you* in geography. There are many candidates who are entered for the examination who are very good geographers but who never quite develop the ability to show this in the examination room. Read on and get involved in the activities to ensure that you are not one of these people.

Using this Revision Guide

This revision guide is not all you need to gain examination success. It has certainly not been written with the intention of replacing your teacher, the most important resource you have.

Most of you will have been studying geography since entering secondary school and will have learned a great deal in that time. You will probably also have notes in exercise books and files that will help you to prepare for your examinations. These notes, and your teachers, are the *real* key to your success in the examinations.

This guide will help you make sense of your own notes. It will also help you use the geographical skills you have learned in answering exam questions. Your teachers will also be working hard with you to ensure your examination success and it is my intention that this revision guide helps in this process.

Unlike many revision guides, it does not contain huge number of facts. These you already have. It does, however, help train you to get the best out of the examination: how to apply your knowledge, understanding and skills.

Features of this Revision Guide

This revision guide contains a number of features intended to help you to *actively* work through your revision schedule – as painlessly as possible! They are highlighted by a number of symbols, each representing a different feature.

Go Active

These activities/tasks help you focus tightly on your revision and will provide an opportunity to test yourself. Be pleased if you do really well. Give yourself a reward. On the other hand, if you find a particular activity a little too challenging, read it carefully again and re-read the section of your notes it is testing. If you still struggle, have a word about it with your teacher.

Inside Information

Sitting public examinations can be quite difficult. Much of this difficulty often results from the fact that many students don't fully understand what the examiner is trying to get them to do or is asking of them. *Inside Information* takes away this mystery to give you an insight into exactly what the examiner wants when using different types of questions.

Exam Spotlight

Exam Spotlight will guide you through exam preparation and strategies for getting the best out of the time you have in the examination room. You will also be given plenty of opportunities to practise with exam-style questions.

Case Study: the Knowledge

You are asked to apply your own knowledge of different places and situations in the Case Study parts of each exam question. How do you make sure you have chosen the right bank of knowledge to answer a particular Case Study? What information is needed from that bank of knowledge? How do you attract top marks for your Case Study answers? These and other questions are explored in *Case Study: the Knowledge* activities.

Getting to know the specification

It is easy to see the examination and, sometimes, your school work as the enemy. It really shouldn't be that way. The specification is written so that your teachers can create a course for you that is both enjoyable and relevant. The examinations are also designed to help you.

The WJEC Geography B Specification

The following is an overview of the three themes that make up the GCSE Geography WJEC B Specification. The key to doing well is to develop an understanding of each of these.

Theme 1: Challenges of Living in a Built Environment	Theme 2: People and the Natural World Interactions	Theme 3: People, Work and Development
• How do quality of life and standard of living differ?	• What are the causes and effects of ecosystem change and how might these be managed sustainably?	• How and why do patterns of employment differ?
• How does access to housing differ, how is this changing and how does it affect people?	• How does the hydrological cycle operate?	• How might development be measured?
• How does access to services differ, how is this changing and how does it affect people?	• What are the causes and effects of drought and how might a sustainable supply of water be provided?	• What are the benefits and disadvantages of an interdependent world?
• Who plans the changing built environment, what conflicts are caused and how might a sustainable built environment be developed?	• What are the causes and effects of flooding and how might it be managed sustainably?	• How do trade and aid operate?
• What are the causes and effects of migration and how might they be managed in a sustainable way?	• How are river landforms produced, how do people use them and how might effects of this use be sustainably managed?	• Where are economic activities located and why are they located there?
• What are the causes and effects of increased use of rural areas and how might these be managed in a sustainable way?	• How are coastal landforms produced, how do people use them and how might effects of this use be sustainably managed?	• What are the causes and effects of changes in the location of economic activities?
		• What are the effects of economic activity on ecosystems and how might these be managed?
		• What are the effects of economic activity on climate change and how might these be managed?

Go Active

Let's make a start. We are going to look in detail at *Theme 1: Challenges of Living in a Built Environment* and you will attempt to match the Case Studies you have covered with the main questions in this theme. You will show yourself where to find the section of your notes that targets each of these questions.

Make a table like the one started below to show coverage of this theme.

1 Fill in the 'Case Study' column.

- Write down the name of the Case Study.
- What's the name of the country in which it is located?
- Is it a country that shows a high or low level of economic development? Write 'richer' or 'poorer'. Sometimes the Case Study question in the examination will demand you use an example from a particular state of economic development.

2 Number the notes you have made during your geography course. This will help you find the relevant parts at a later stage rather than wasting valuable revision time searching for them. In the 'Page Number' column make it clear exactly where you can find the notes about this part of the specification, e.g. 'Exercise Book 3, pages 15 to 18'.

3 Briefly outline the main points of each Case Study you have included. Perhaps bullet points would be useful. These statements will help you recall the greater detail you have in your notes. This should make life a little simpler in the examination room.

4 When you have completed this table you may wish to create your own for the other two themes. Simply copy the questions from each of the other themes, then follow steps 1 to 3 again.

As you can probably imagine, this is something that is best done as you go through your course. Don't leave everything until the last minute!

Questions	Case Study	Page Number	Main Points
How do quality of life and standard of living differ?			
How does access to housing differ, how is this changing and how does it affect people?			

Assessment through WJEC Specification B

The examination jigsaw: piecing it all together

When you actually sit the different parts of the overall examination is a decision you and your teachers will make. The only certainty is that it will be in the summer. It is possible that you will sit one part of the written examination in Year Ten and the other in Year Eleven, though equally possible that you will sit both parts in Year Eleven. In some schools you may even sit part of it in Year Nine. There are no hard and fast rules.

In a similar way, the two parts of the assessment called 'controlled assessment' must be completed by March in the year that you take your final examination. This is, basically, your coursework. When you attempt these is likely to be decided by your teacher; he or she is the best person to judge what time will be most appropriate for you.

The other decision that will be made by you and your teacher is at what level you will be entered, either the Foundation or Higher Tier. It is actually possible to combine Foundation and Higher Tier entry to give you your final grade.

The big picture

Whichever parts of the assessment you sit and whenever you sit them, the different components or elements of the overall assessment are shown in the following table.

Name	Nature of assessment	Time	Proportion of total mark
Controlled assessment	I The enquiry	maximum 8 hours	15%
	2 The issue	maximum 5 hours	10%
Unit I: Foundation or Higher tier	Theme I	I hour	15%
	Theme 2		15%
Unit 2: Foundation or Higher tier	Theme 3	30 minutes + I hour 30 minutes	15%
	Problem-solving		30%

EXAM SPOTLIGHT

The finer detail
- Each large area of content is called a 'Theme'.
- Each theme is tested through the two 'Units' or examinations.
- Unit 1 tests Themes 1 and 2.
- Unit 2 tests Theme 3.
- Unit 2 also tests your ability to solve a geographical problem.

Inside Information

Foundation or Higher Tier – the facts

- You can get a Grade C by either route.
- The Higher Tier exams place greater demands on your language skills.
- The Foundation Tier exams organise your answers more for you.
- Entry by the Foundation Tier route is not a sign of failure.
- Most students will enter both units at Foundation Tier or both at Higher Tier. However, if you take Unit 1 in Year Ten at Foundation Tier, and then make lots of progress in Year Eleven, you can be entered for the Higher Tier of Unit 2. In this case, your grade could be higher than a C if you do well.

Making your mind up

- Consider your level of entry early in your course.
- How might this triangle help you decide?

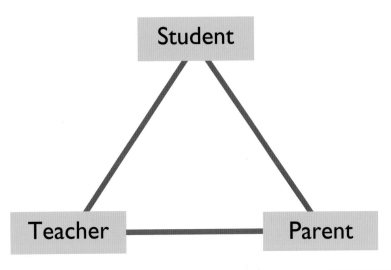

Making the exams work for *you*

It's worth shouting out loud, *'your examiners really want you to do well'*. They use quite a few different methods to help you provide them with the answers they want. This can only happen, though, if you play their game.

There are three key rules:

1 Read all the information provided on the examination paper. There may be no questions to answer on its front page, for example, but there are instructions and other information to help you.

2 Manage your time carefully. You must actually *complete* the paper if you are to do well. Your examiners help you by telling you how many marks are available for each question and by giving you the number of lines they feel you will need for your answer.

3 Do everything that is asked of you. Your examiners use 'command terms' to tell you what sort of answer they want. These words always mean the same thing so you must always respond to them in the same way. Practise this throughout your course.

Go Active

The table gives the main command terms that will be used in your Geography exam. It also gives their meanings. Your task is to match each term to its meaning.

When you have finished, check your answers with the list on page 15. Only when you have finished, though!

Command term	Meaning
1 Circle	**A** Give an *accurate* figure by reading a graph or map. Do not just give an estimate.
2 Complete	**B** Create a sketch map or diagram to help explain a feature, describe a location or show your plans for an area.
3 List	**C** Place a circle round the correct answer from a list of alternatives.
4 Name	**D** Say what is similar and/or different between two pieces of information.
5 Locate	**E** Similar to 'explain' but expects you to provide the information from your own knowledge rather than using that provided by the exam paper.
6 Measure	**F** State where a place is.
7 Draw	**G** Explain why you have made a decision.
8 Describe	**H** Write down more than one feature from looking at a map, photo or other resource.
9 Explain/Give reasons for	**I** Fill in gaps on something like a graph or in a sentence.
10 Suggest	**J** Just write what a feature is, e.g. the 'motorway M6' on an OS map.
11 Compare	**K** State why something you have described exists or has happened.
12 What is meant by	**L** Just write exactly what a feature or place is e.g. 'Black Stone' or 'a bridleway'.
13 Justify	**M** Give a definition of a geographical term.

Effective revision

The only person who can decide how to revise most effectively is you. There are a huge variety of techniques and some will suit some people more than others. Perhaps the following questions will help you to decide your most effective method of revision:

- Do you need complete silence to revise?
- Does music help to cut out outside noises?
- Can you concentrate for long periods of time?
- Is your attention span short?
- How many different exams do you have?
- Where is geography in the exam timetable?
- What parts of your social life are essential?
- What can you give up to make time for revision?

There is just one rule when answering these questions – be totally honest with yourself. There is a very long period of time between your examinations and results day. You will only enjoy this time fully if you have thoroughly prepared yourself for the examinations and can honestly say that you could not have tried harder.

So, now you are armed with this vital information, create your own customised revision programme that:

- starts early enough
- balances work and pleasure
- suits your concentration span
- is realistic in the demands it places on you
- takes place in conditions that suit you
- builds in rewards.

Finally, remember just three more points:

- Your teacher is there to help and will welcome questions.
- There may be geography lessons offered during your study leave time – attend them!
- Everyone realises the pressure you are under. If you feel, at any time, you are not coping be sure to talk to someone about it.

Inside Information

Are you naturally untidy? If so, train yourself in the art of keeping tidier notes. If your work is in exercise books, number them and write a brief content record on the inside front cover of each book. Create something similar for loose-leaf notes and don't forget to number the pages. If you don't do this, a dropped ring binder depositing its contents on the floor could be very troublesome.

Go Active

On page 12 there is a revision timetable. Two copies of it will give you a plan for a twelve-week revision period. Complete this to focus your revision activities. Use marker pens or simple ticks to track your progress.

Revision timetable

	Week 1 & 7 Date:	Week 2 & 8 Date:	Week 3 & 9 Date:	Week 4 & 10 Date:	Week 5 & 11 Date:	Week 6 & 12 Date:
Monday						
Tuesday						
Wednesday						
Thursday						
Friday						
Saturday						

Active revision

Your revision can be either active or passive. Passive revision involves just reading your notes and is something that is likely only to work over very short periods of time. After this the mind begins to wander and all sorts of outside influences will get in the way of effective revision; things like staring at posters on your wall or listening to noise coming from outside your room.

On the other hand, active revision involves you actually *doing* something. This is likely to help you maintain your concentration at a reasonably high level and can often result in you producing something that will be helpful later in the revision process.

There are a number of activities you could do.

- Make revision cards for the main Case Studies you hope to use in the examination. Divide each card into areas for separate features of the Case Study.
- Link features affecting or influencing a particular aspect of a Case Study by drawing spider diagrams or webs. This is useful for things like the influences on quality of life of, for example, local service provision or the effects on an area of a river flood.
- Create cards to test yourself and your friends on some of the key terms needed for success in a Geography examination. Produce one set of cards containing the terms and another set with their definitions. Use them as a simple matching exercise or a game of Geography 'snap'. You might also consider creating a set for each of the three themes.
- Well drawn sketch maps and diagrams are always welcomed by your examiners. Try to memorise some of these and then attempt to re-draw them. Compare your re-drawn map with the original.

Each of these strategies for revision success is looked at in greater detail as you work through this book.

And finally …

The big day has come, you have revised well and there is nothing that can get in the way of your success. Or is there?

Think about the following to help you stay in control of the situation. You should:

- reach the exam room in plenty of time
- listen carefully to your invigilators
- know your centre and candidate number
- carry spare writing equipment
- read front page instructions
- use your time well
- answer all questions – don't leave gaps
- carry a *small* mascot – if any!

Go Active

Discuss the points in the checklist above with friends, teachers, parents.

How will each point help you stay in control?

Are there any other ideas that will help you?

EXAM SPOTLIGHT

- The questions you will need to answer have been designed by the examiners to encourage you to show your geographical abilities as fully as possible.
- Some words will be in bold while others will be italicised.
- You may wish to highlight other words yourself to help you understand exactly what the question is asking of you.
- Look at the question on the right. A candidate has underlined the words she thought important to her full understanding of the question. The messages she got from each area of highlighted text are given in the speech bubbles.

> Description is not enough. I must also give reasons for the damage.

> I can't write about any landforms. This is quite specific.

> A tight focus. I must write only about how the damage is caused and not stray into attempts to prevent it.

Explain how coastal or river landforms may be damaged by the people who visit them. You may use ideas from areas you have studied.

> Good. This is an invitation to use information from case studies I have worked on in class, read about or seen on TV.

Go Active

You may not agree with the underlining of the candidate. You may also feel that highlighting using a marker pen would be more useful to you.

1 Attempt the same task on copies of the questions below.

2 Write a brief description of the message given to you by each piece of text you have highlighted. You may find the information above helpful.

'Suggest and explain advantages and disadvantages of building on greenfield sites.'

'Explain how fair trade might help poor countries with their development.'

'Describe and explain the possible effects on the water cycle of converting a small lake into a large reservoir.'

'Compare the purposes of short term relief aid and long term development aid.'

Common command terms explored

Describe

Just write what you see. You will normally be asked to describe a photo, graph or map. Look at the mark to work out how much detail you need to give. Remember, do not explain anything in these questions.

What is meant by

You are being asked to define a geographical term. You need to learn the key terms and definitions. Use the Glossary in your textbook to help you. Don't give an example instead of a definition; the examiners want to know that you have understood what the term means.

Explain/Give reasons for

These questions test your knowledge and understanding. You are being asked to say *why* something you have already described is happening. Use 'because' to help you answer these questions.

There are often 2 marks awarded for giving just one reason. For these questions, you will be expected to give a simple statement and an elaboration. To write the elaboration, ask yourself 'So what?'.

Suggest

This is similar to 'Explain' but tells you that you are expected to bring in ideas and understanding of your own. Therefore, the ideas required are not provided in the exam paper.

Compare

When you see a question asking you to compare, you should write what is similar *and* what is different between two pieces of information. You should make use of words like 'whereas' and 'in contrast' to help you make comparisons.

Measure

You may be asked to measure something on a map or graph. Don't guess – measure accurately using the scale provided.

So what? The art of elaboration

Many questions ask you to demonstrate more depth of geographical understanding than a simple statement can show.

For example, when you are asked to give two reasons for an event taking place and there are four marks available the question is actually asking you to give two simple statements each followed by an elaborated 'so, therefore … '.

Try to complete each sentence below by following it with at least one 'so what?'. The first one has been done for you.

- Mains sewerage is usually not connected to squatter settlements in LEDCs so drinking water supply is contaminated *so people suffer water-borne diseases*.
- Large shopping centres have developed on the edges of British cities so
- Many office workers now use the internet to work from home so
- Much electricity production relies on burning quantities of fossil fuels so

Answers for Go Active: Command words (page 10)
1C; 2I; 3H; 4J; 5F; 6A; 7B; 8L; 9K; 10E; 11D; 12M; 13G

Challenges of Living in a Built Environment

How do quality of life and standard of living differ?

Many factors affect people's quality of life. Some, but not all, of these can be measured. The amount of money you own, for example, may be measured but the effects of your friends can not.

Happiness, well being and satisfaction of a person.

Quality of life

?

Standard of living

Housing, possessions and income of a person.

Go Active

Complete a copy of the spidergram in Figure 1 to show what affects your quality of life:

1 School and home are listed on the spidergram. Show how these affect you in both a positive and negative way. Use different colours.

2 Add other influences to your spidergram.

3 Add cross links between the main influences.

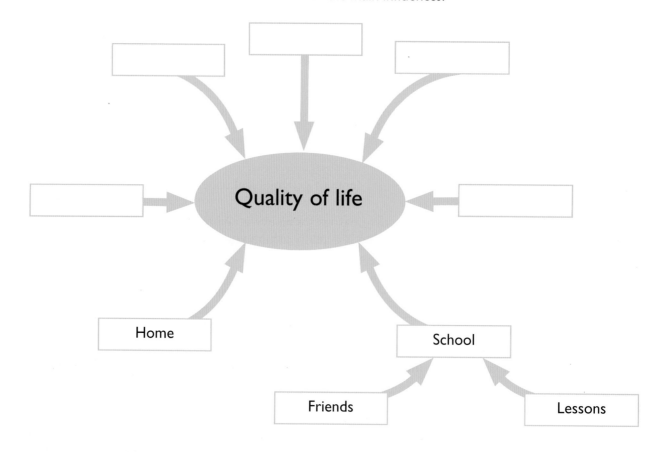

Figure 1 Quality of life spidergram

Study Figure 2.

- **List three** features in the photograph that could affect the quality of life of these people.
- **Suggest** how each feature may affect their quality of life.
- **Compare** your quality of life with that of these people.

Figure 2 Influences on quality of life, rural Ghana

Inside Information

- Look carefully at the command terms in the Exam Spotlight above (in bold). Check their meanings on page 15. Only give what is asked for.

- Learn key terms – for example, what is the difference between rural and urban? Your examiners expect you to know certain terms in the examinations.

Go Active

1 Choose two of the indicators in Figure 3.

2 Explain how each of these shows that people living in Ghana are likely to have a poorer quality of life than people living in the UK.

3 Which of the definitions at the top of page 16 refers to quality of life and which refers to standard of living?

	UK	Ghana
Life expectancy at birth (years)	79	59
GDP per capita (wealth) $US	33,238	2,480
Adult literacy % (15 years+)	99	58

Source: Human Development Report, 2009

Figure 3 Standard of living indicators: UK and Ghana, 2005

How does access to housing differ, how is this changing and how does it affect people?

Access to housing

Where do people live? There does seem to be an obvious answer to this question but think about the area around your school. What differences are there in housing types? Are there groups of similar types and sizes of houses, or are they mixed up? Who owns the houses?

Housing types include detached, semi-detached, terraced or town houses and apartments. They may range from those that are very large to those that are very small. Where these different types of housing are found is often quite varied and depends on how settlements have developed with time. Sometimes simple patterns can be seen, although some settlements like London are too big to show them.

	Central Business District (CBD)	Inner City	Inner Suburbs	Outer Suburbs
Cost of Living	High	Low	Medium	High/Low
Housing Types	Apartments	Old terraced blocks 1960s high rise flats and low rise houses Modern town houses	Mixed detached and semi-detached houses	Large detached houses, 1960s high rise flats and low rise houses
Ownership	Owner occupied Privately rented	Owner occupied Council rented Privately rented	Owner occupied	Owner occupied Council rented

Figure 4 Possible pattern of housing types in a large town or city

Different housing may also be suited to different groups of people. The needs of a single person, for example, are quite different from those of a family with two children. People's housing needs also tend to change with time.

Go Active

1 Look at the cross section in Figure 4. Describe how housing type changes from the CBD to the outer suburbs.

2 Draw a section to show similar changes in your nearest town or city.

3 Use information from Figure 4 to help you explain the changes on your own section.

4 How do these changes compare with the section above?

5 To what extent would you get a different pattern if you drew a section in a different direction from the CBD?

Ownership of housing is also quite varied:

- Some are owned outright by the people who live in them, or they are paying off a loan called a mortgage from a bank or building society. This housing is said to be **owner occupied**.
- Some people rent their home from a **social landlord**. This is a landlord who does not make a profit. There are two main types:
  - Some people pay rent to the local authority. This is sometimes described as **council rented**.
  - Some people rent from a **Housing Association**.
- Similarly, in some forms of housing the occupier pays rent to a private individual who owns the property. This is called **privately rented**.
- Existing housing is sometimes occupied illegally, or houses are sometimes built illegally on land that is not owned by the builder. This is **squatter** housing.

Go Active

1 Look at the descriptions of the three families below.

A young couple with no children yet. They have a high combined income and a large mortgage. They both work in city centre offices and live in a city centre apartment.

A family of four, including two children under five. There is one wage earner and they have been refused a mortgage to buy a house. They rent a council owned high rise flat in the suburbs.

An elderly couple living in a five bedroom detached house in the outer suburbs. They no longer own a car.

2 For each family, make a list of advantages and disadvantages of living in their current houses.

3 Which family is in the most suitable type of accommodation?

4 How might time change their needs?

5 Why do people not always live in the housing most suited to them?

Housing in many poorer countries

The pattern of housing is just as complex in poorer countries as it is in the UK. However, again there are some general patterns that may be applied:

Centre			Suburbs
Central Business District	**High quality**	**Low quality**	**Squatter**

- There is as wide a range of quality of housing, as in the UK.
- A smaller proportion of people live in high quality houses and apartments.
- A greater proportion are either homeless and sleep on the streets, or live in squatter settlements.
- Lots of squatter housing is distributed close to the city centre or along main arterial routes.

Features of the town or city that may disrupt the basic pattern from centre to suburbs include:

- main roads
- rivers
- railways
- industrial areas.

Squatter settlements

These have a variety of names including favela, shanty towns, spontaneous and informal settlements. Whatever the name, they are unplanned and are built on land that does not belong to the residents. They consist of any scrap materials that can be freely found and usually lack basic amenities like:

- a piped water supply
- mains sewerage
- street lighting
- paved roads
- a source of electricity.

Go Active

Suggest how each of the following factors is likely to influence where a squatter settlement will grow:

1 Most people living in squatter settlements move into the city from the countryside.

2 Water is important for drinking, cooking and washing.

3 It can be expensive to commute to work.

4 The rich live near the city centres.

5 Squatters have little access to private transport.

6 Flood plain land tends to be avoided by formal housing.

What's in an image?

You see images everywhere, in newspapers, school textbooks and television for example. They are mainly snapshots of a moment in time and are sometimes selected by the user to put over a particular idea to the reader or viewer. In both your piece of coursework called the 'Issue' and the 'problem solving' examination you will be exposed to different viewpoints often backed up by images.

EXAM SPOTLIGHT

1 Draw a sketch of the photograph in Figure 5a.
2 Label it to show features of this housing which affect the quality of life of the people living in it.
3 Annotate your sketch to show how these features affect their quality of life.

Figure 5a The Algarve, Portugal; not all low quality housing is in poorer countries

Figure 5b Street scene, Gaborone, Botswana

Go Active

Briefly describe Figures 5a and 5b and the photograph on the front cover of this book (a market scene from a market in Accra, the capital of Ghana).

1 What feelings does each photo give you about the place?

2 What images would you use to show your own local area in:
   - a positive way
   - a negative way.

3 Explain your choice of images.

Inside Information

- You may be asked to add information to a sketch of a photograph.
- Information that describes what you see is called 'labels' and information that helps explain something is known as 'annotation'.
- It may be useful to practice labelling and annotating using different colours to distinguish between the two.

How does access to services differ, how is this changing and how does it affect people?

It's not just the house or housing area we live in that affects our lives. Our quality of life is also influenced by the services we have access to. The availability of these will also depend upon where we live.

What services do you use and how do they affect your quality of life? Ones that directly affect you on a daily or weekly basis include school, shops, sport and recreational opportunities. Others are perhaps only noticeable when you need to use them. These include such services as hospitals and doctors' surgeries.

Services are often found in particular parts of built up areas. In fact, some show quite definite patterns. There is a definite pattern of shopping services within a city or large town, for example. This pattern has developed and changed over time as our urban areas have grown and changed. The old pattern of terraced houses in inner-city areas is being broken down and as these have been replaced, many corner shops have disappeared. On the other hand, increased travel opportunities, brought about by improved public transport services and increased car ownership, have encouraged the growth of suburban supermarkets and huge out-of-town shopping centres. Home deliveries and use of the internet are also now having a major effect on our shopping patterns.

Having services in a particular area is important. However, far more important than that is the ease at which people are able to access them; either by choice as with shopping and entertainment, or need in the case of an emergency.

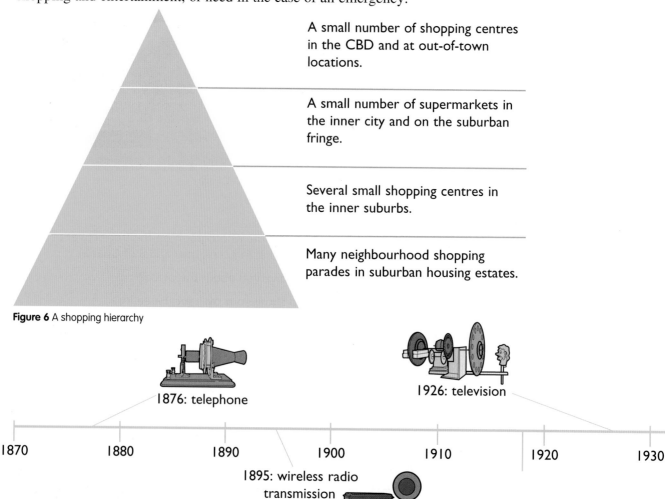

A small number of shopping centres in the CBD and at out-of-town locations.

A small number of supermarkets in the inner city and on the suburban fringe.

Several small shopping centres in the inner suburbs.

Many neighbourhood shopping parades in suburban housing estates.

Figure 6 A shopping hierarchy

1876: telephone

1926: television

1870   1880   1890   1900   1910   1920   1930

1895: wireless radio transmission

Figure 7 A technological timeline

Go Active

1 Look at the section in Figure 4 on page 18. Photocopy it and use the information from Figure 6 on page 22 to add each type of shop to its correct place on the section.

2 Based on the services they wish to use, suggest one part of the city on the section where the people described below may best live.

3 Explain each of your choices.

4 Why is the choice of where to live not quite so simple?

An elderly couple, not car owners, who are mostly happy to stay at home but go to the city centre and local supermarket to shop.

A mother of two young children. She is off work on maternity leave and needs to do a regular shop for perishable goods.

A teenager whose interests include supporting the local football team and going to the cinema.

A keen golfer with no access to private transport.

Go Active

1 Look at the timeline in Figure 7.

2 Describe briefly how the timeline has changed communication.

3 Explain how the changed communication on the timeline has enhanced your quality of life.

4 Suggest negative effects of the changes.

1966: satellite television

1980: laptop

1980: cross-border mobile network

1940   1950   1960   1970   1980   1990   2000

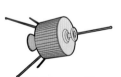 1969: internet   1975: personal computer   1995: mp3 player

Who plans the changing built environment, what conflicts are caused and how might a sustainable built environment be developed?

Who really makes the decisions that affects our lives? How much say in changes to your area do you or your parents have? To what extent does the real power rest in the hands of a small number of people? Can you really influence their decisions?

The main players in a traditional urban planning decision are shown in Figure 8.

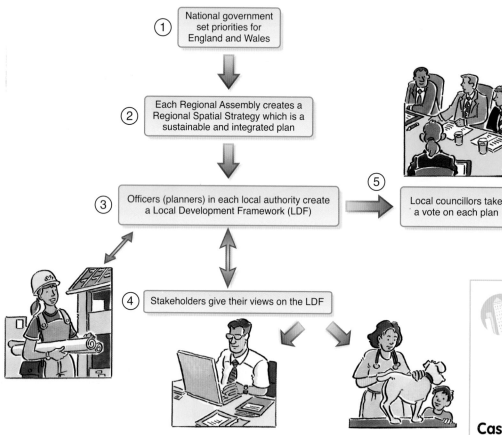

1. National government set priorities for England and Wales

2. Each Regional Assembly creates a Regional Spatial Strategy which is a sustainable and integrated plan

3. Officers (planners) in each local authority create a Local Development Framework (LDF)

5. Local councillors take a vote on each plan

4. Stakeholders give their views on the LDF

Figure 8 The three tiers of decision making in the planning process

Go Active

1. Describe the planning process in Figure 8.

2. Who appears to have the most power?

3. Look at Figure 9 on page 25. Which five of the eleven 'standards' of an eco-town do you think are most important?

4. To what extent do you think this approach to planning is breaking away from the traditional planning model?

Eco-towns

Eco-towns are new communities currently being planned that will accommodate between 5000–15,000 homes, green spaces, schools, health care facilities, businesses and shops. Each will look to showcase the best of our new green technologies and will be built to the highest level of design.

Case Study – the Knowledge

Where is your nearest planned eco-town? Look it up on the internet. Use the information you find online and the information in Figure 9, to plan an answer to the following Case Study questions:

1. Name an area of planned change.

2. Describe its location.

3. Explain how the change may affect people and the environment.

A different approach? A UK Government web-based survey on eco-towns

The information in Figure 9 is based on a government sponsored website. You can go straight to the website http://ecotownsyoursay.direct.gov.uk/my-eco-town/what-should-it-look-like/ or use the information provided below.

Each of the standards represents an important aspect of creating an eco-town. You must decide which of the standards are important to you. On the website you would be asked to select the five you consider to be the most important.

Standard 1 – Building the eco-towns

We want to make sure eco-towns are thriving communities from day one.

That means making sure transportation, decent infrastructure and public services are as important as housing.

This standard will ensure that people will have easy access to the quality services they need.

Standard 2 – Giving the community a voice

People living in eco-towns must have a say in how things are run.

Every eco-town must have a long-term structure run by residents to make sure that developers meet the right standards and that they are upheld in the future, and a plan for how they will involve the community in important decisions.

Standard 3 – Achieving zero carbon

Over a year, net carbon emissions from all energy used in buildings in eco-towns must be zero or less.

Developers will need to show how they will achieve this.

Standard 4 – Transport

Eco-town residents should be able to get around easily without relying on their cars.

Eco-towns should give priority to walking, cycling and good public transport – at least half of all trips should be car-free. And homes should be within a ten minute walk of frequent public transport as well as neighbourhood services.

Standard 5 – Homes

Homes in eco-towns should have real-time energy monitoring to show families how much energy they are using and how much they are spending.

Homes should also have high speed broadband and live information on public transport.

Eco-towns will have at least 30 per cent housing affordable to low wage earners.

Standard 6 – Employment

Eco-town residents should be able to work in their community. Plans should support job creation and business development – especially jobs which are easily accessible without a car.

At least one job per house, on average, must be easily reached by walking, cycling or public transport.

Standard 7 – Local services

Families who live in eco-towns will enjoy a healthy, vibrant community – including leisure, health and social care; education, retail, culture and library services; sport and play, community and voluntary sector facilities.

Standard 8 – Adapting to climate change

Eco-towns should be built with climate change in mind and resilient to future changes in climate so that residents have confidence for the long term.

Standard 9 – Water & floods

Water efficiency is very important for eco-towns to safeguard and protect the availability of this resource.

Care will also need to be taken when planning buildings to protect people from the risk of flooding.

Standard 10 – Green space

There must be at least 40 per cent green space in an eco-town. And at least half of that must be community space. Plans should have a range of quality green spaces, for example community forests, wetland areas and town squares.

Special focus should be given to land for growing food locally such as community gardens and allotments.

Plans also need to show how wildlife and natural environmental features will be protected for people to enjoy.

Standard 11 – Waste

Eco-towns must reduce waste and recycle substantially more than the national targets, as well as make use of waste in new ways, e.g. fuel.

Figure 9 A UK Government web-based survey on eco-towns

What are the causes and effects of migration and how might they be managed in a sustainable way?

Migration is the movement of people from one place to another in order to live. The people who move are called migrants. Migration may be from one place to another within the same country or it could be international, from one country to another. Migration takes place for a number of push and pull factors. Push factors are those aspects of an area which encourage people to move away. Pull factors are features of an area that attract people.

Figure 10 Potential push and pull factors

Urban to rural migration

A feature of some richer countries, such as the UK, is the movement of people from urban to rural areas. In other words, people migrate from the cities to villages in the countryside.

Some influences that encourage people to migrate from urban to rural areas include their perceptions of:

- air pollution
- congested roads
- clean air
- fear of crime
- empty roads
- friendly community.

Villages fighting back?

People who migrate to rural areas often have different needs from those who are already there. The newcomers often commute to work in nearby towns and cities and then use the services they find there. They also pay high prices for houses, leaving young villagers unable to afford housing in the village and, as a result, forcing them to move away.

The Campaign to Protect Rural England (CPRE) is concerned about these housing issues, but is also worried that the migration of outsiders into villages poses a threat to local services:

'CPRE believes that rural services such as post offices, banks, local shops, schools, buses and pubs, play a vital role in the economies and communities of rural areas. It is in all our interests to ensure that we have a countryside where people can have access to services nearby. Local services improve the quality of life and bring environmental benefits such as reduced travel and lower traffic levels.'

(CPRE, Policy Statement, March 2006)

Go Active

1 Look on page 6 at the six influences on migration from urban to rural areas.

2 Complete a copy of the table below.

3 Add two influences of your own.

EXAM SPOTLIGHT

Urban push	Rural pull	Explanation
Air pollution	Clean air	Concern about health effects of breathing air polluted by vehicles in city. Perception of much less impact in villages.
Fear of crime		
Congested roads		

If you are asked in the examination to give two reasons why people migrate from one area to another do not give a matching pair. For example don't quote 'air pollution' and 'clean air' from the table above.

Instead, give two completely different reasons, for example, 'air pollution' and 'fear of crime' in the cities.

Go Active

Use the CPRE statement to complete the following exam question:
(a) List two village services the CPRE wishes to preserve. [2]
(b) Give one reason for each of these two services to explain why it is likely to disappear from the village. [4]
(c) Explain the effect of its closure on local people without private transport. [4]
(d) The CPRE feel that keeping village services will help the environment. Explain why they think this. [4]

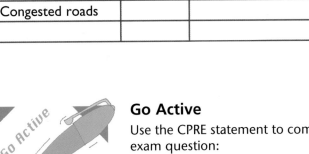

Inside Information

Consider the following ideas when answering the question above:
(a) You are only asked to list. All you need to do is write the names of two services from the CPRE article. Don't write more. Don't name services that are not in the article.
(b) There are two marks for each reason, so you will need to elaborate your response here. For example, if you choose 'buses', it is not enough to say that 'More people travel by private car'. You will need to add a 'so what?' statement like, 'so less demand for public transport means a reduced or no service.'
(c) and (d) In each of these questions you have a choice of answer. Neither question tells you how many reasons you need to give so you could give a variety of answers in these ways:

Statements	Marks
Four simple statements without any elaboration	4 x 1
One simple statement with three connected elaboration or 'so what?' statements	1 + 1 + 1 + 1
Two simple statements. One having two connected elaboration or 'so what?' statements	1 + (1 + 1 + 1)
Two simple statements, each having one connected elaboration or 'so what?' statement	2 x (1 + 1)

Rural to urban migration

The push of the countryside

In many of the world's poorer countries the migration is from rural to urban areas. Living conditions pushing people away from the countryside are likely to include:

- the poor quality of everyday life brought about by lack of work
- no school in the village
- a great distance from medical help
- an unreliable supply of water.

A response to disasters

Although living conditions may be very difficult in some areas, the final decision to migrate is often made when a disaster strikes, for example a flood or a drought. Some of the most devastating disasters are the result of problems brought on by people.

Zimbabwe

Millions of migrants crossed the border from Zimbabwe into Limpopo Province of South Africa in the early 2000s. For several years the country has been poorly managed with high unemployment and rapid inflation, making it difficult for people to live there. Some of the migrants are official asylum seekers or economic migrants with work permits. Most, though, are informal migrants who have no documents. They have moved mainly through desperation but also with the aim of sending money back to help family who remain in Zimbabwe.

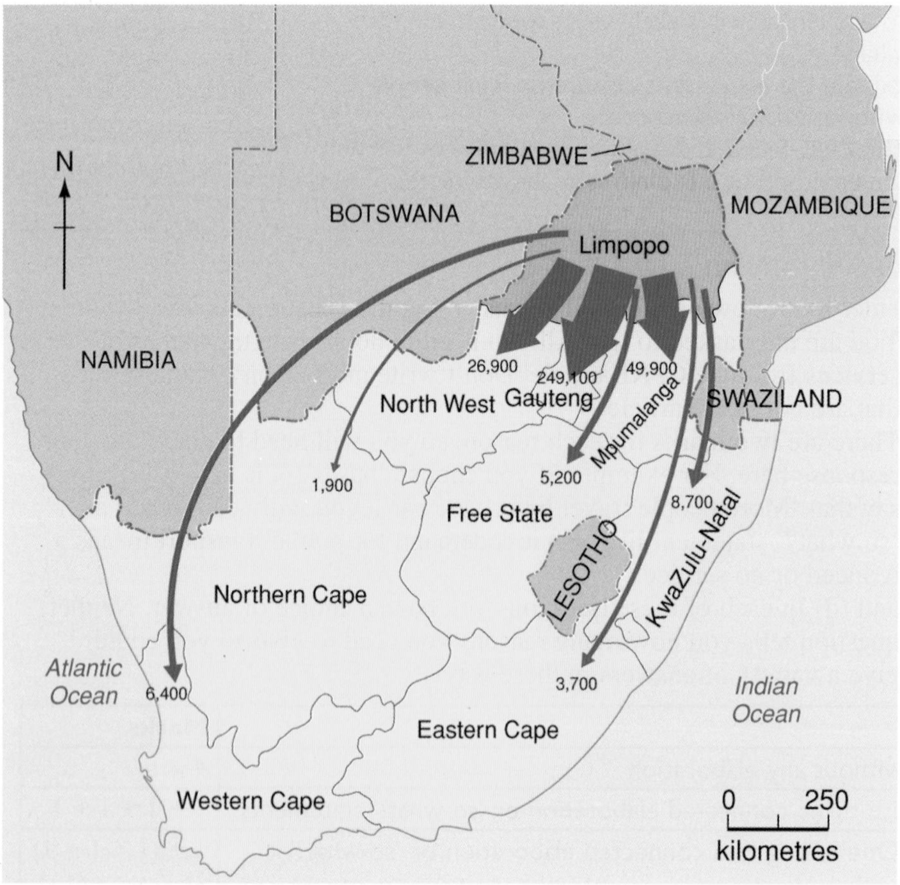

Asylum seeker: has a well-founded fear of persecution in their country of origin for reasons including political opinion, religion, ethnicity, race/nationality, or membership of a particular social group.

Economic migrant: moves from one country to another for work or other economic opportunities.

Figure 11 Migration from Limpopo Province during 2005

Go Active

Complete a copy of the table below to show how living conditions have a negative effect on people's quality of life in some rural areas. Use the four living conditions from the previous page and add a fifth one of your own.

Rural living conditions	Effect on quality of life
Lack of work	
No school in village	(so) children can't read and write (so) don't get well paid jobs.
A great distance from medical help	
Unreliable water supply	

Go Active

1 Read the information about Zimbabwe.

2 What is the difference between an asylum seeker and an economic migrant?

3 Suggest how the South African government might feel about informal migrants. Explain your view.

4 Many migrants stay close to the South Africa/ Zimbabwe border. Why might this happen?

5 Use the map in Figure 11 to help you describe the pattern of movement of migrants from Limpopo Province to the rest of South Africa.

Inside Information

A question that asks you to use a map to describe patterns is quite common in the examination. When answering one make sure that you:
• describe the general pattern
• give exceptions to the general patterns
• use accurate figures.
Make sure that you do *not* offer explanations for the patterns you have described.

Go Active

1 Read the news article below about the effects of migration on children.

2 List ways in which a Zimbabwean child's life in a village is likely to be different from your own.

Effects of migration on children

Social conditions in Zimbabwe, like many African countries, are changing rapidly. Many heads of households are migrating away from the rural areas to the cities. This, though, is often a staging post on the way to a new life in South Africa. The migrants are often young adults, the most productive members of the family. These movements are made more damaging by the fact that in some cities the proportion of people who are HIV positive is around 25 per cent. Many are incapable of looking after their families.

The bottom line is that many households are now being run by the eldest child. It is almost impossible for these 'heads of households' to gain the education they so desperately need. They can't go to school when their time is mainly taken up with the adult responsibility of feeding their younger brothers and sisters. They are being forced to grow up far too quickly.

Those whose parents have migrated live in hope that they will return richer than they left or that they will send home regular payments to keep the family in food and shelter. Sadly, this doesn't happen very often.

Source: Stuart Currie

The reality of migration in poorer countries is rarely as good as the expectations, either on the journey or when they get to their final destination.

Figure 12 A young lone migrant

The pull of the cities

People are pulled to the cities by the perception of a better life. They are attracted by the positive reports of people who have left the village before them and expect to find all those features missing from their lives in the countryside.

The reality

Migrants rarely find the housing or the job they are seeking. Much employment is informal and housing is likely to be a slum dwelling (see page 21) at best. Many migrants sleep on the streets.

Pressure on the city authorities

A large influx of people into an urban area is likely to put a great deal of pressure on the town or city authorities. They will need to react to demand for jobs, education, healthcare and housing.

In many cities the authorities have worked with squatters to provide them with a brick-built one- or two-roomed house, a piped water supply, mains sewerage, an electricity supply and a small garden. These are also provided with paved roads and street lighting. Such communities are known as site and service schemes.

Go Active

Look at the photo of the young migrant in Figure 12. Life for migrants like this may be described as being dangerous. Explain why.

Go Active

1 Draw a sketch of a brick-built house and label it with the features of site and service dwelling.

2 Explain how each feature is likely to provide a better quality of life for the residents than the squatter dwelling they previously lived in.

Case Study

Attempt this Case Study question based on your own knowledge of migration into an urban area.

For a migration into an urban area:
(a) Name and locate the urban area.
(b) Describe the urban housing conditions experienced by the migrants.
(c) Explain why the migration took place.

Inside Information

- Your Case Study answers are marked using a 'levels of response' mark scheme. It awards you marks according to the quality of your answer rather than the number of points you make.
- Your answer should fit into one of the levels in the mark scheme.
- When you have answered the Case Study on migration, use one of the mark schemes to check it.
- Through the Case Study, your examiner will also be marking the quality of your spelling and grammar.

Foundation Tier

Level	Description/Explanation
1 1–2 mark	Choice of case study applied reasonably well. Gives simple description or explanation.
2 3–4 marks	Appropriate choice of case study applied well. Gives descriptive points with some explanation.
3 5 marks	Appropriate choice of case study applied very well. Provides a balanced account which includes specific description and explanation.

Higher Tier

Level	Description/Explanation
1 1–2 marks	Gives basic, generic description and/or explanation.
2 3–4 marks	Appropriate case study named. Provides an account which includes some specific description and/or explanation.
3 5–6 marks	Appropriate case study applied well. Provides a balanced account which includes elaborated description and explanation.
4 7–8 marks	Appropriate choice of case study applied very well. Provides a sophisticated account which includes specific and wholly accurate description and explanation.

What are the causes and effects of increased use of rural areas and how might these be managed in a sustainable way?

Many people live longer now and workers have more holidays than in the past. This all adds up to more leisure time. People can also move from place to place more speedily and cheaply, so we can travel further to enjoy ourselves. Surely, this can only be good news? Not always so (see Figure 13)!

Figure 13 Conflict in the countryside

Too many visitors?

Pressure on areas of outstanding natural beauty can not only cause conflict between the different users, but can also damage the very environments we wish to visit.

Niagara Falls is a honeypot site. It attracts people in huge numbers to see and hear half a million gallons of water plummeting over the falls every second. About 6 million tourists come to see it each year. To cater for the tourists, the area has been filled with hotels and restaurants and many people earn a living from these.

Figure 14 Niagara Falls

Honeypot site: a place that attracts many tourists. At peak times, they may be very crowded and congested. They risk being spoiled by the noise and litter of the visitors.

Go Active

Look at the cartoon in Figure 13, which shows conflict in an area of natural beauty.

One example of this is conflict between farmers and hikers in the area. The cartoon shows that some hikers leave farm gates open, which allows animals to escape onto the road. As a result, the farm animals could be killed or injured by motor vehicles, which in turn would cost the farmer a loss of earnings.

	Farmer	Hiker	Motorist	Picnicker	
Farmer		✔			
Hiker					
Motorist					
Picnicker					

1 Place two more ticks on a copy of the table to identify other areas of conflict. For each conflict you have identified, explain the reason for it.

2 Add another possible user of the valley to your table and explain how this person could add to the conflict.

Inside Information

You may be asked to use a labelled and annotated sketch or sketch map in the examination. You, therefore, need to know the difference between labelling and annotating.

Labelling is just writing what is there, while annotating is explaining something about the feature you have labelled.

For example, you will label the dual carriageway by just using the two words 'dual carriageway' but you will annotate it by writing something like 'makes it easier for visitors to drive around the area'.

Go Active

Look at the photograph of Niagara Falls (Figure 14) and then look at Figure 15.

1 Label a copy of the sketch to show the following: The Falls, hotels, dual carriageway, café.

2 Annotate the sketch to show how each of the features you have labelled could attract visitors.

3 Suggest how the popularity of Niagara Falls has made it a less attractive place to visit.

Figure 15 Tourist pressure at Niagara Falls

Creating and sustaining rural communities

Protecting areas of natural beauty

The pressure suffered by some areas of natural beauty has long been recognised and special powers have been given to authorities in order to protect them from the activities of people. The most protected of these areas are called National Parks. The world's first National Park was created at Yellowstone in the USA in 1872. The first National Park in England and Wales was the Peak District National Park set up in 1951.

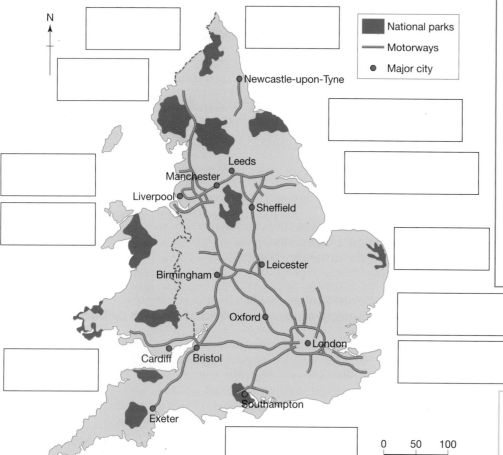

Figure 16 National Parks of England and Wales

The National Parks of England and Wales have three aims:

- To conserve and enhance the natural beauty and cultural heritage of the National Park.
- To promote opportunities for public enjoyment and understanding of the special qualities of the National Park.
- To foster the economic and social well-being of communities living within the National Park.

Go Active

Use an atlas to help you label a copy of Figure 16 to show the names and location of each National Park.

EXAM SPOTLIGHT

Attempt this exam question using the map on this page and the page opposite.

(a) Compare the distribution of English regions having a high percentage of second homes with the distribution of National Parks. [4]

(b) Suggest and explain two reasons for the distributions you have described. [4]

Inside Information

When asked to compare, you must say how things are similar and different to each other. Using words like 'similarly' when there is a positive correlation and 'whereas' when there is a negative correlation will help you do this.

Second homes – an issue facing National Parks

Figure 17 The percentage of homes in hamlets and isolated villages that are unoccupied because they are either second homes or rented out as holiday homes

Key
10% and above
5–9.9%
2–4.9%
0–1.9%

0   50   100
kilometres

The village of Brendon in the north of Exmoor National Park is an ideal bolt-hole for city dwellers. Huddled in the picturesque wooded East Lyn valley, close to Lorna Doone country, red deer and open moorland, it is easy to understand why many come here to escape the stress of the office. But now up to 40 per cent of properties in the village are second homes, standing empty for much of the year.

That may soon be about to change. Exmoor wants to stop local people being priced out of the housing market by blocking outsiders from buying second homes. The park authority, which intends to convene within a month to vote on the matter, would be the first national park to impose such a ban.

Exmoor will consider insisting on a change of use for properties that are occupied for less than six months of a year in parishes where more than 10 per cent of properties are second homes. At the same time it will insist that every new building and conversion must be sold to those working or living in the park, or who have had local connections for 10 years.

Source: *The Independent Online,* Mark Rowe and Catherine Peppinster, 11 August 2002.

Go Active

1 Read the three comments below.

2 Each comment relates to one of the three aims of National Parks. Match the comment with the aim it relates to.

3 With which aim do you most agree? Explain your choice.

4 With which aim do you least agree? Explain your choice.

Free talks on the geology of the National Park should be offered to visitors.

Areas should be closed to visitors to prevent any more footpath erosion.

A new quarry should be allowed to open inside the National Park.

Inside Information

You are likely to be asked to give your opinions in both examination papers. Make sure that you justify the points you make by fully explaining why you hold your viewpoint. You will already have had practice at this throughout your course and in the 'Issue' part of your Controlled Assessment.

Go Active

1 Read the article from *The Independent.*

2 What attracts people to Brendon?

3 Suggest the effect on the area of 40 per cent of property being second homes.

4 How is the Exmoor National Park Planning Board attempting to meet its third aim?

People and the Natural World Interactions

What weather and climate results from high and low pressure systems?

Weather: Day-to-day changes in the atmosphere.

Climate: Average weather conditions over a period of, usually, at least 30 years.

Inside Information

Weather and climate – don't confuse these two terms. It is quite possible that a Case Study question might ask you to explore one or the other. When asked for a 'climate type' it would be rather foolish to write about the European heatwave of August 2003, or the effects of a severe depression like a hurricane. These are both weather events. Be careful!

Depressions and anticyclones

A large amount of information is continually recorded at weather stations around the world. Data collected includes precipitation, temperature, wind speed and direction, sunshine and atmospheric (air) pressure.

Air pressure is used to build up synoptic charts (weather maps) that show the positions and nature of low and high pressure areas. The centres of low pressure are called **depressions** and the centres of high pressure are called **anticyclones**.

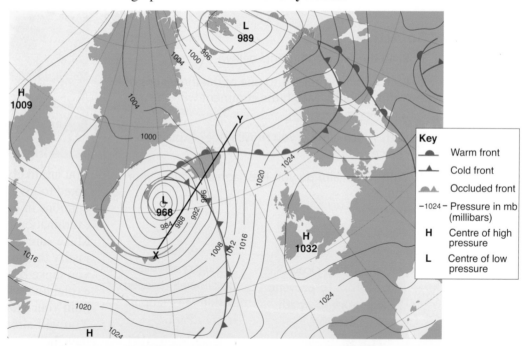

Key

Warm front
Cold front
Occluded front
−1024−	Pressure in mb (millibars)
H	Centre of high pressure
L	Centre of low pressure

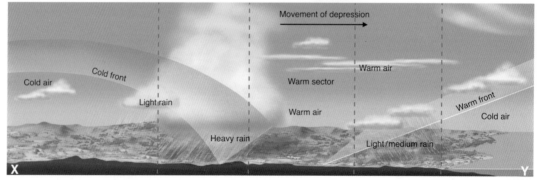

Figure 1 Weather map and section showing a deep area of low pressure in the North Atlantic on 4 September 2003

Go Active

Use information from Figure 2 to label a copy of the weather map (Figure 1).

1 Add the following labels:
   - depression
   - anticyclone
   - rising air
   - falling air.

2 Add arrows to show the air circulation.

3 Add a bold arrow to show the movement of the depression.

Feature	Depression	Anticyclone
Air pressure	Low: usually < 1000 mb	High: usually > 1020 mb
Vertical air movement	Rising	Falling
Wind strength	Strong	Weak
Wind circulation	Anticlockwise	Clockwise

Figure 2 Main features of depressions and anticyclones

Go Active

The section in Figure 1 shows the different weather experienced as a depression passes. Rearrange the following text boxes to show the sequence of weather at Point Y as the depression moves.

Thick cloud Heavy rain Cold	High cloud Little or no rain Cold	Lowering cloud Rain Cold	High, light cloud No rain Warm	Cloud and sunny intervals Showers Cold

Go Active

In a depression rain falls as air rises at a front (frontal). It can also rise as a result of the air being heated by the earth (convectional) or being forced over mountains (orographic). In each case the following process takes place:

air rises ⇝ it cools ⇝ cool air holds less water than warm air ⇝ water vapour in the air condenses ⇝ clouds form ⇝ precipitation occurs

EXAM SPOTLIGHT

Complete the following question:

(a) What was the name of the pressure system over the UK on 4 September 2003? [1]

(b) Explain why no rain falls here. [3]

(c) Suggest and explain two ways in which the weather it brought may have affected the lives of people. [4]

How do anticyclones and depressions affect people's activities and quality of life?

Everyday life

On the last page you were asked to explain how an anticyclone in early September might affect people's quality of life. The clear skies will encourage air temperatures to rise quickly during the day, which could possibly result in weeks of hot and dry weather. This may have both a positive and negative impact on quality of life; outdoor sports as well as ice cream and cold drink sales may increase, but pressure might be applied to water supplies and healthcare services.

The effects of winter anticyclones are quite different. There is no cloud blanket to retain heat, so in these situations, clear skies result in very cold conditions with severe frost and, often, the formation of thick fog. Effects on people could include the cancellation of outdoor sports due to frozen pitches and hazardous travelling conditions due to ice and fog. Conversely, brighter days combat Seasonal Affective Disorder (SAD) and hot drink sales might increase.

We experience events like these and those that happen with the passage of depressions on a regular basis. It is when weather events become severe that the real problems occur.

Severe weather events

A cyclone is a severe depression. They are also called hurricanes. Cyclone Nargis hit southern Myanmar in early May 2008. The story of Nargis is shown below.

Nothing has yet been said about how people respond to major disasters like this one. That comes under 'aid' and is addressed in Theme 3: People, Work and Development.

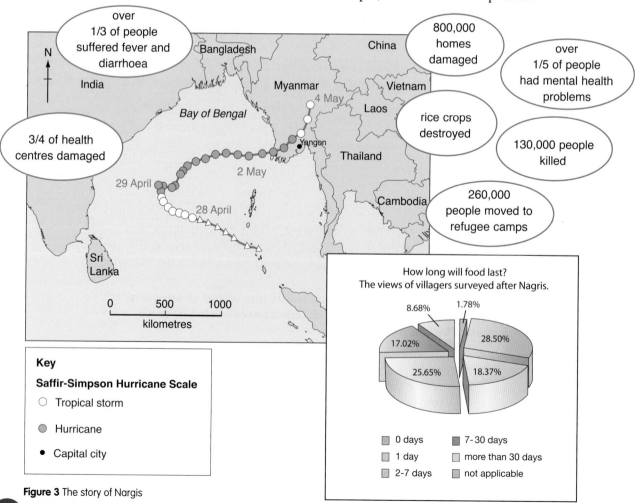

Figure 3 The story of Nargis

EXAM SPOTLIGHT

Use Figure 3 to complete the following questions:

(a) Describe the path taken by Cyclone Nargis between 28 April and 4 May, 2008. [3]	In this question you will gain marks for detail as: • describing the direction and changes in direction of the path of the cyclone • stating when it changed from tropical storm to hurricane category and back again • stating when it reached land.
(b) Describe what the graph shows about the impact of Cyclone Nargis on people's diet. [3]	Marks are awarded here for your detailed reading of the graph, so include accurate figures. Note those elements of the diet that hardly changed, those that decreased the most and the one that has increased.
(c) Choose three ways in which the cyclone affected the lives of people. For each way you have chosen, explain the effects. [6]	All of the marks in this question are for your explanation. The different ways are given to you in the boxes surrounding the map and graph. For example: Choice: over 1/3 of people suffered fever and diarrhoea. Explanation: people put pressure on healthcare services [1] so many are not treated and die. [1] Select your three ways from the six that remain.

Go Active

Look at the photo in Figure 4. It shows an area of farmland in the Trent valley during a winter anticyclone.

1 Suggest ways in which these weather conditions might affect the everyday life of a farmer.
2 Compare this with the way the weather conditions would affect a typical day in your life.

Figure 4 Farmland in a winter anticyclone

Go Active

Complete a copy of this table to show the conditions brought to the UK by different types of weather events.

Weather event	Conditions	Positive impacts	Negative impacts
Depression			
Summer anticyclone			
Winter anticyclone			

The hydrological cycle

How does the hydrological cycle operate?

Water may be stored or flow between stores. It is found in three states: liquid, solid and gas.

Store: Where water remains in one place and state.

Flow: The transfer of water between stores. This could be in the same state or involve a change of state.

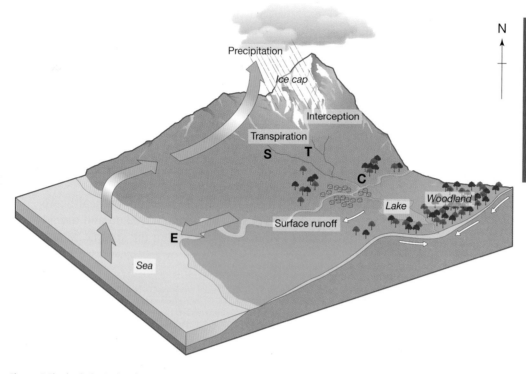

Figure 5 The hydrological cycle

Figure 5 shows part of a river's catchment area. This is the area from which it receives all of its water. Catchment areas are separated from each other along watersheds, which are ridges of higher land.

Human interference

Most of the land area of the UK has been directly affected by the activities of people. For example, urban areas are largely covered by buildings and other impermeable structures. Rural areas, however, are dominated by vegetation, although much of this has been planted or is managed by people.

The nature of the surface has a major effect on how water falling onto a drainage basin returns to the rivers and, eventually, the sea.

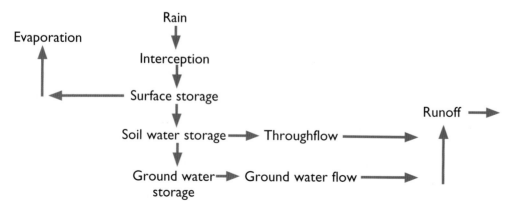

Figure 6 Rural discharge

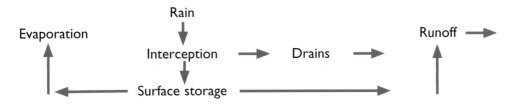

Figure 7 Urban discharge

Most of the water that falls on rural areas does so onto fields, moorland and woodland. Many of these surfaces are permeable, so much of the water infiltrates the ground. The situation is quite different in urban areas. Here, much of the water falls onto impermeable concrete or tarmac surfaces, along with the roofs of buildings. However, drains carry it quickly to the rivers.

Go Active

Attempt these two matching exercises to revise some important terms.

1 Each of the letters on Figure 5 shows a feature of a drainage basin. Link each with its description:

A Confluence (C)	I where a stream begins
B Tributary (T)	2 where two rivers join
C Estuary (E)	3 a small river feeding into a larger one
D Source (S)	4 where a river enters the sea

2 This is a more complex exercise. It asks you to link the names of the main flows of the hydrological cycle with their meanings. Another name for the hydrological cycle is the *water cycle*.

A Precipitation	I water seeping into the ground
B Interception	2 transfer of water from a liquid to gas
C Evaporation	3 movement of water through the soil
D Transpiration	4 water falling out of the atmosphere
E Infiltration	5 movement of water through rocks
F Throughflow	6 transfer of water vapour from vegetation
G Ground water flow	7 where falling water hits the Earth's surface

EXAM SPOTLIGHT

Attempt this two-part question.
Look at the diagrams showing discharge rates (Figures 6 and 7). Discharge is the way in which water that lands on the Earth's surface returns to the sea. The rate of discharge varies according to where the water falls:
(a) Compare the discharge in rural areas with that in urban areas.   [3]
(b) Which rate of discharge is likely to be faster? Explain your choice. [4]

Inside Information

These are two separate questions. In the first part of this question you are being asked to make a comparison. Begin by stating what discharge is like in a rural area, then state how urban discharge compares with it. You may wish to outline both similarities and differences. When writing about the differences, use terms like 'whereas', 'but' or 'in contrast'.

You are not being asked to explain anything until the second part of the question. Start the second part by giving your choice of 'urban' or 'rural' (1 mark). The sequence of your answer should then be: simple explanation (1 mark) + so what? (1 mark) + so what? (1 mark).

What are the causes and effects of flooding?

Causes and effects

You have already seen two causes of flooding. Increased urbanisation results in water reaching the rivers much more quickly, which in turn increases the risk of flooding. Also, as global warming causes sea levels to rise, some coastal areas are likely to flood more frequently.

> **Lag Time**: The time between the peak in a period of rain and peak discharge of the river.

> **Discharge**: The volume of water flowing down a river. It is measured in cubic metres per second (cumecs).

> **Bankfull Stage**: The discharge above which the river will be unable to hold all of the water, so floods.

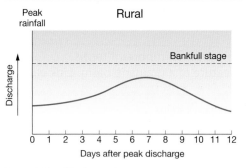

Figure 8 Flood hydrographs

Some parts of the world are more naturally prone to flooding than others. For example, deltas like those of the Ganges in Bangladesh and the Mekong in Cambodia and Vietnam. Both of these deltas are affected by a 'Cyclone Season'. Look back to pages 38 and 39 for the effects of cyclones.

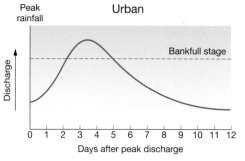

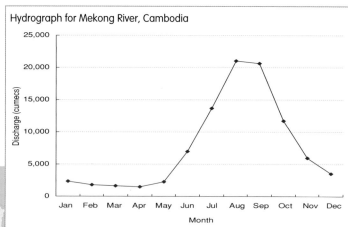

Type of loss	Mekong Delta
Human	30 people died
Assets	1400 houses destroyed; 23,864 houses inundated; 164 education rooms damaged and 101 classrooms moved
Fisheries	1100 hectares fish and shrimp ponds damaged; 852 fish cases damaged and 29 tonnes of fishery lost
Transportation	19 km national roads, 705 km rural roads, 140 bridges
Water control structures	185 units damaged, 104 km embankment eroded
Others affected	5 provinces
Total cost	US$1.5 million

Figure 9 Flooding of the Mekong delta

The 8th Annual Mekong Flood Forum

The 8th Annual Mekong Flood Forum, held on 26–27 May 2010 at the Don Chan Palace Hotel, Vientiane, Laos, discussed the issue of international co-operation in helping fight flooding along the river. The activities of countries in the upper river area can have a great effect on water control in the river's lower course.

For example, a dam built in China in the upper course could have the following impacts:

on the upper course
- safer water supply
- cheap electricity
- economic growth
- greater water control

on the lower course
- drop in water levels
- water release from dam causes flash floods
- reduction of fish
- less water control

Go Active

1 Produce a 'fact file' on the Mekong flood or any other flood you have studied. Then attempt tasks 2–7 to explore the issues surrounding international co-operation on flood control.

Include information on:
- the location of the flood. Draw a sketch map to show it
- the main causes of the flooding
- the effects of the flooding on the lives of people.

When completing this last bullet point, you will need to give 'so what?' statements in relation to people's lives. Look back at page 39 for some help.

2 List in order from source to mouth the countries through which the river Mekong flows.

3 Which countries have the least control over the flow of water?

4 Why, in times of flood, is it important for these countries to have the co-operation of those in the upper course of the river?

5 How might dams in the upper course be used to help reduce flooding in the lower course?

6 Write two brief statements from spokespeople for:
- a country in the lower course explaining why help is needed in times of flood
- a country in the upper course explaining why it is difficult to help.

7 Why is international co-operation very difficult?

We will look further at sustainable management of flooding in the 'Problem solving' chapter on page 80.

How does drought affect people?

What is drought?

'An extended period during which an area receives less rain than would normally be the case.'

In other words, it is not an actual figure in millimetres but a relative one in which people and ecosystems have to cope with much less rain than they would normally receive: a difficult situation to be in!

How does drought affect people in richer countries?

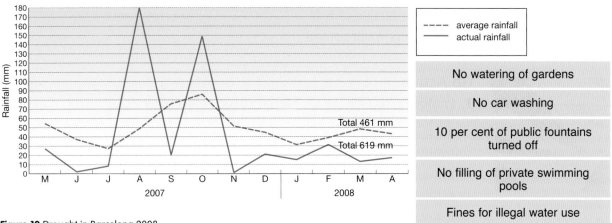

No watering of gardens

No car washing

10 per cent of public fountains turned off

No filling of private swimming pools

Fines for illegal water use

Figure 10 Drought in Barcelona 2008

Attempt one of the following sets of questions:

Higher Tier
(a) Describe the pattern of precipitation between May 2007 and May 2008. [3]
(b) Compare this with the average precipitation. [3]
(c) Explain how the precipitation pattern in 2007 and 2008 affected the quality of life of people in Barcelona. [4]

Foundation Tier
(a) Complete the following passage:
'Average precipitation varies between a low of 27 mm in _____ and a high of _____ mm in October. There is also precipitation in all months. In contrast, the actual precipitation shows two months with none at all: July and _____ .
Differences between high and low are much greater, with a maximum precipitation of _____ mm greater than average in October 2007. The actual precipitation was lower than average in _____.' [5]
(b) Give, and explain two ways in which people's quality of life was affected by the drought. [4]

Inside Information

The Higher and Foundation Tier examinations differ from each other in a number of ways. In many instances they place different demands on your geographical abilities. However, on other occasions, questions in both Tiers are written differently but still ask you for similar geographical information. In the question above, the Foundation Tier question is more heavily structured to support the candidate in providing the correct geographical answers, whilst the Higher Tier question gives the candidates more freedom to structure their own response.

How does drought affect people in poorer countries?

The area bordering the southern edge of the Sahara Desert contains some of the poorest countries in the world. The ways in which people living there respond to drought differ significantly from responses in the richer world.

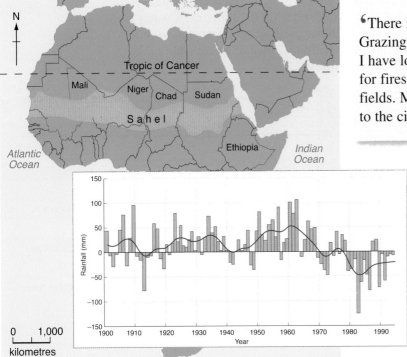

Figure 11 Annual rainfall anomalies in Sahel countries 1900–95. Each bar represents whether the total rainfall in each year was above or below average. The line shows the trend

'There is little water in the well. Grazing for my goats has dried out and I have lost many animals. Even wood for fires is scarce. Crops just die in the fields. Many of my friends have moved to the city.'

'My hut is on the edge of town and I take my turn at the shared tap. Water is only supplied for 8 hours a day and the queue is long. The water pressure is so low that it takes a long time to fill my large container. Dysentery and other water-borne diseases are common in this neighbourhood.'

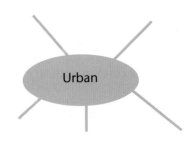

Go Active

Use a plain A4 sheet to help you access the information about changes in the Sahel.

Set it out like this:

Location

- Continent of Africa.
- *North to south depth?*
- *East to west extent?*
- *Countries affected?*

Rainfall change since 1900

- Fluctuated above and below average.
- *Highest: how high and when?*
- *Lowest: how low and when?*
- *Changes in trend with time?*

Effects

Use the webs below to help you organise effects on life in the urban and rural areas. You may wish, instead, to attempt this for a different drought Case Study you know.

No water in well.
So what? Water dirty and rationed.
So diseases and dehydration.
So death.

Rural

Urban

How might a sustainable supply of water be provided?

International co-operation

It is not just annual climatic change and rainfall variation that causes problems with water supply. Particularly in richer countries, we have increased our demand for water. Meeting the increased demand sometimes relies on the transfer of water from one place to another, often across country boundaries. Any such transfer would be via a series of pipes and canals from areas with a surplus of water (more than enough) to those having a water deficit (too little).

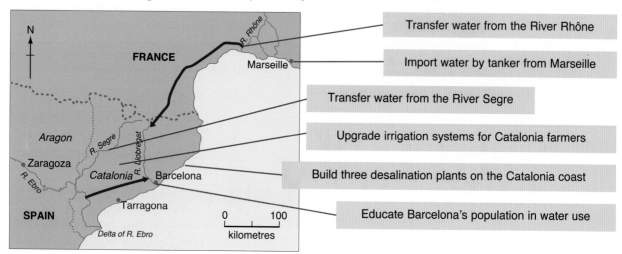

Figure 12 Meeting Barcelona's water needs

Go Active

Look at the information on Barcelona's water supply in Figure 12.

1 Make two lists: one of solutions that will help provide a sustainable water supply in the future and the other of those that you feel are unsustainable.

2 For each solution, explain why you feel it is either sustainable or unsustainable.

How big should a scheme be?

Governments in many of the world's countries have developed large-scale, multi-purpose water schemes. These schemes involve damming major rivers to create huge lakes.

They have a number of advantages and disadvantages:

Advantages	Disadvantages
Prevention of flooding	Drowning of settlements under the lake
Provision of water for farms and houses	Reduction in natural supply of fertiliser to farmland
Generation of electricity	Reduction of water supply further down river
Attraction of secondary industry	Destruction of land and river habitats
	Expensive to set up and operate

Go Active

1 Using a multi-purpose water scheme you have studied, add specific detail to the list of advantages and disadvantages on page 46.

2 On balance, do you feel that the scheme you have studied should have been developed? Why?

Appropriate technology – a more sustainable option?

In some poorer countries, governments and non-government organisations (NGOs) like WaterAid, are setting up small-scale schemes in farming villages.

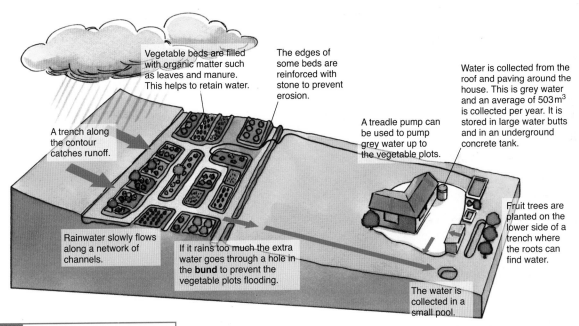

Vegetable beds are filled with organic matter such as leaves and manure. This helps to retain water.

The edges of some beds are reinforced with stone to prevent erosion.

Water is collected from the roof and paving around the house. This is grey water and an average of 503 m³ is collected per year. It is stored in large water butts and in an underground concrete tank.

A trench along the contour catches runoff.

A treadle pump can be used to pump grey water up to the vegetable plots.

Rainwater slowly flows along a network of channels.

If it rains too much the extra water goes through a hole in the **bund** to prevent the vegetable plots flooding.

Fruit trees are planted on the lower side of a trench where the roots can find water.

The water is collected in a small pool.

Figure 13 Rainwater harvesting in South Africa

EXAM SPOTLIGHT

Study the diagram in Figure 13.

(a) List three ways in which this scheme gets maximum use out of available water. [3]

(b) Give and explain two ways in which this scheme may be considered sustainable for a small farm. [4]

Inside Information

● In part (a) you are asked only to list and your response is worth only three marks. To describe in detail would gain no extra marks and would only waste your ink and, more importantly, time.

● However, you *are* asked to give a detailed explanation in part (b). Think about the scale of operation, the amount and type of power needed to operate it and the simplicity or complexity of the machinery used.

How are landforms produced?

Agents of erosion

It doesn't matter whether you're thinking about coastal landforms or those created by rivers, they are both formed due to processes of erosion, transport and deposition. Although they create different types of landform along coasts or rivers, each of these processes operates in a similar way.

Hydraulic action: The breaking up of rock material caused by water compressing air in cracks within rock surfaces, before releasing it explosively. Also known as *quarrying*.

Abrasion: The wearing away of rock surfaces by pieces of rock held in the water. Also known as *corrasion*.

Corrosion: The dissolving in water of soluble rock material, like limestone (calcium carbonate). Also known as *solution*.

Attrition: The wearing down of rock material by fragments rubbing together during transport.

Figure 14 Agents of erosion

Differential erosion

Where rocks of different resistance are found together, erosion differs according to the resistances of the different rocks.

Figure 15 Differential erosion at Etretat, N France

Weaknesses in the headlands will be exploited by wave action. Agents of erosion will combine to produce caves. Eventually, caves on either side of the headland will join to form an arch. With further erosion the arch will eventually collapse to form a stack.

Go Active

1 Look at all of the information on page 48.

2 Draw and label a copy of Figure 15 to show how erosion operates on a headland to produce caves, arches and stacks.

3 Alternatively, do the same for a different headland you have studied in class.

Inside Information

When a Case Study question asks you to explain the formation of a landform, the examiner expects you to explain using a sketch of an actual example, rather than a diagram that could be of anywhere.

See what you make of the question below.

Case Study – the Knowledge

Read the following passage:

The Niagara River flows over a resistant horizontal band of limestone: the cap rock. Beneath this is a much less resistant layer of shale. The force of water undercuts the shale and eventually the limestone cracks and breaks until, under the force of gravity, it collapses. Collapsed limestone rests in front of the American Falls. The falls slowly erode back to leave a gorge through which the river flows.

(a) Draw a sketch of the photograph (Figure 16).

(b) Add labels at the end of the arrows to show:
- limestone cap rock
- less resistant shale
- collapsed limestone blocks
- Niagara gorge.

(c) Add arrows and labels to show the locations of:
- two areas of undercutting
- a plunge pool.

(d) Suggest how the area will change in the future.

Do you have an example of a different landform that could be used to answer the question above? If you do, use the exercise above to practise.

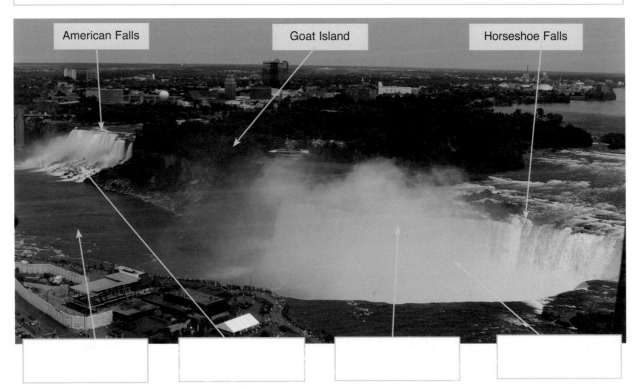

Figure 16 Gorge formation at Niagara

Transport and deposition

When a river, or the sea, has broken up the rock it moves the fragments to another place. When the energy is too little to move the fragments, they are deposited. These processes are known as transport and deposition.

Transport

Water transports material in four different ways:

Solution: This consists of rock material dissolved in water. It may eventually become solid again if the water evaporates.
Suspension: Material 'floats' in the water as it moves.
Saltation: Material is bounced along by the moving water.
Traction: Material is rolled or dragged along. It doesn't leave the surface as it is carried.

In the last three methods, the size of material that is carried will depend upon how quickly the water is moving. Fast moving water will carry heavier material than water that is slow moving.

Coastal transport and deposition

Some material eroded from the coast is carried away from the shore and deposited at a distance. However, a large proportion of material is transported along the coast by a process known as longshore drift. As it rests, it produces a number of features of deposition. These include beaches, spits and also bars with lagoons behind them.

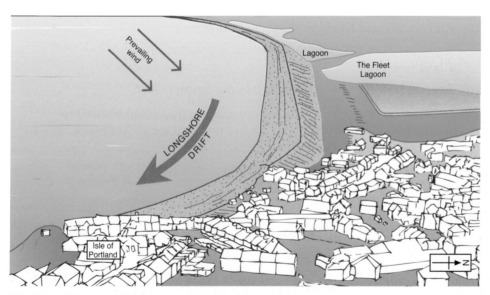

The swash carries beach material up the beach in the direction of the prevailing wind.

The backwash carries beach material back into the sea at right angles to the shore.

A lagoon forms when fresh water is prevented from reaching the sea.

Key
▨ Chesil Beach

Figure 17 Longshore drift on the Dorset coast

Go Active

1 Use the information in Figure 17 to label a copy of it with:
   - arrows to show movement of beach material up the beach
   - arrows to show the return of this material to the sea
   - the names 'swash' and 'backwash'
   - a lagoon other than Fleet Lagoon.

2 Using information from your sketch, explain how longshore drift operates at Chesil Beach. Include place names and the compass directions of beach material movement in your explanation.

River transport and deposition

Unsurprisingly, rivers transport material in the same way as the sea. After all, they are both moving bodies of water. Thus, solution, suspension, saltation and traction carry material down rivers too.

It is in the lower course of the river that the gradient, and therefore the speed of the water flow, reduces. As this happens, carried material is dumped or deposited. This helps form two important features of the lower course.

Meanders

Figure 18 A meander on the River Severn

Go Active

Draw a sketch of Figure 18. Use information from the passage below to label different parts of your sketch.

'A meander is a large bend in a river. The speed of water flow is greater on the outside of the bend; here the banks are eroded to form a river cliff. Water speed is much slower on the inside of the bend; here deposition takes place. The deposited material forms a low mud or sand bank: a slip-off slope. In times of high rainfall or snow melt, the river reaches bankfull stage and overflows its banks. Material deposited on the valley floor creates the river's flood plain.'

Flood plains and people

Go Active

Complete a copy of the table to show the physical qualities of flood plains and the effects of these qualities on the lives of people. Attempt to add at least one item in the quality column.

Quality	Effects on the lives of people	So what?
The land is flat.	Easy to use farm machines on it.	Speeds up farming activities and reduces the need for labour, cutting the farmer's costs.
River material deposited each year.	Provides a natural source of fertiliser.	
No barriers to movement.		
Often floods.		
Soil often very wet and heavy.		

Interfering with natural processes

Can we prevent coastal erosion?

Many people live in places that are vulnerable to such natural processes as flooding and erosion. Property worth large amounts of money is often threatened. In these cases, it is difficult for people to insure against their losses.

In some places, groups of people, often local governments, have implemented schemes to try and control the negative effects of such natural processes, such as coastal erosion.

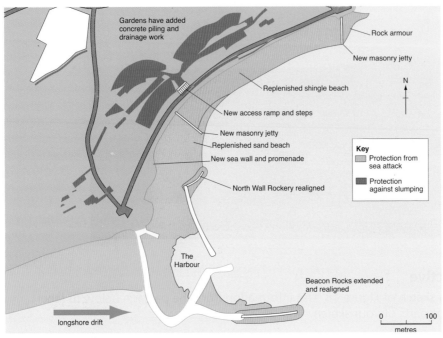

Figure 19 Protecting an area of coast – Lyme Regis, Dorset

Go Active

1 Complete a copy of the table below to match processes that may have taken place before the protection scheme was put in place and places they could have happened. One has been done for you.

Process	Place
1 Heavy rain saturates the cliff causing landslips	In areas where beach replenishment is needed
2 The sea erodes the bottom of landslips	Old sea wall areas now replaced by new walls
3 Coastal defences undermined by the sea	On the coast beneath slumped areas
4 Eroded material and beach sand is carried away	Places inland now protected from slumping

2 Write numbers 1 to 4 in suitable places on a sketch of Figure 19.

3 Annotate your sketch to suggest effects of the following:

- The new jetty.
- Replenishing the beaches.
- Drainage work on the cliff.
- Renewing the sea wall.

Protecting one area of coastline usually causes problems for people living further along the coast in the direction of longshore drift. In the case of Lyme Regis, longshore drift is prevented by the new jetty but the coast to the north-east could be starved of new supplies of sand. Meanwhile, the sand which is already there is carried further to the east by longshore drift. The effect of this could be a beach starved of sand like that in Figure 20. In the short term this is likely to put property in the unprotected area at risk. In the longer term the unprotected cliff could erode so far back that it could also expose the protected part to erosion.

Figure 20 Starved beach to the north-east of Lyme Regis

EXAM SPOTLIGHT

Attempt this set of questions:

(a) Describe two features of the beach in Figure 20. [2]

(b) Describe two features of the cliff. [2]

(c) Complete each of the following sentences to help explain the state of the coast in the photo: [3]

  (i) Sand carried in a downdrift direction has not been replaced, *so* …

  (ii) The beach is lowered in height, *so* …

  (iii) The undercutting of the weak cliff is now more rapid, *so* …

(d) Describe and explain the likely effects on the following: [4]

  (i) people living close to the unprotected area of coast

  (ii) people living close to the protected area of coast.

(e) Some people think coastal protection is sustainable. Others disagree. With which view do you agree? Describe and explain the possible consequences of ignoring this view. [5]

Inside Information

Question (e) asks you to give your own informed opinion. There is no correct answer, so you will gain credit for the *quality* of your response. As before, the response will be marked using a levels mark scheme. Make sure that your answer targets the highest level, as indicated below:

Levels of response marking. Work upwards through the levels.

Foundation Tier	Mark
Response insufficient for Level 1	0
Level 1: Gives a simple description.	1
Level 2: Gives simple explanation that is lacking in detail	2
Level 3: Gives detailed explanation	3/4

Higher Tier	Mark
Response insufficient for Level 1	0
Level 1: Gives only description.	1
Level 2: Gives detailed explanation	2/3
Level 3: Gives detailed explanation that is place specific	4/5

People, Work and Development

How and why do patterns of employment differ?

Work: people's activities that don't involve leisure. The work may be paid or unpaid; you are doing unpaid work at the moment for example.

Employment: Work for which some form of pay is given.

Go Active

Complete a table for yourself and another member of your family, similar to the one below:

Me	Work (W) or Employment (E)	Family member	Work (W) or Employment (E)
Homework	W		

Now look at the types of employment. What is the main type of employment in your table?

Employment types

There are three main types or sectors of employment:

Primary: growing or extracting raw materials.

Secondary: manufacturing and processing goods.

Tertiary: providing a service.

The proportion of each of these sectors varies depending on the specific place and also the specific time period to be studied.

Generally, in less economically developed places, more people will be employed in primary, rather than secondary or tertiary, industry. This same pattern also applies to currently richer countries the further back in time we go. The development of farm machinery reduced the need for manual labour within the primary sector. Similarly, more recent advances in computerised factory machinery have meant that less manual labour is required within the secondary sector.

Go Active

Look at the following nine jobs. There are three examples each of primary, secondary and tertiary employment. Which jobs fit into each sector?

farmer   steelworker   fisher   teacher   miner

nurse   car assembler   secretary   silicon chip maker

Study Figure 1.
(a) Give two differences between the pie charts.   [2]
(b) Explain what these differences suggest about Malaysia's development between the two years.   [2]

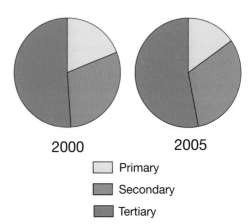

2000   2005

☐ Primary
■ Secondary
■ Tertiary

Figure 1 Employment in Malaysia: 2000 and 2005

Gender and age issues

Employment is not always fair. People are often treated differently according to whether they are male or female, or according to their age.

> **Girls in poorer countries are less likely to go to school than boys**

> **There are over four times as many male than female UK Members of Parliament**

> **In some poorer countries, boys as young as 8 work long hours in unsafe factories**

Figure 2 Unfair treatment?

Go Active

1. Look at the news headlines in Figure 2.

2. Explain how each may affect the quality of life of individuals and groups of people.

3. Suggest what might be done to make each situation fairer.

Go Active

1. Explain the following differences between the two years shown in Figure 3:

   • a rise in females in tertiary industry in both countries

   • a much larger reduction of both females and males in primary industry in Malaysia.

2. Add two more differences shown by the graphs and suggest why they exist.

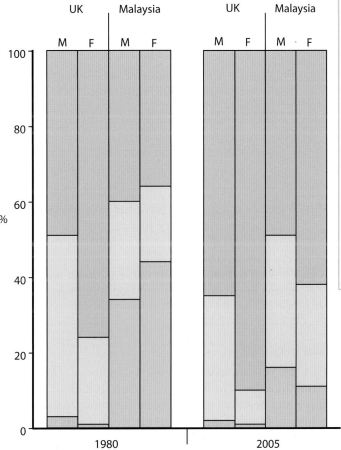

Figure 3 Shifts in employment by gender

Inside Information

You will be expected to respond to factors that influence the lives of people. In the examination, it is quite likely that you will be asked to talk about how a particular factor might affect a person's quality of life. When answering such questions, it is useful to try and put yourself in the position of the person or group affected… and don't forget to use some 'So what?' statements!

How might development be measured?

The measure of development most often used is wealth. It is often given as the Gross Domestic Income (GDI). This is the value of all final goods and services made within the borders of a country in a year. Sometimes this amount is divided by the country's population to give the GDI per person or 'per capita'.

Let's take an extreme example. A country of just four people has a total earnings of $40,000. The GDI of that country would be $40,000 but its GDI per person would be: $40,000 ÷ 4 = $10,000.

Gross National Income (GNI) is almost the same as GDI but is worked out slightly differently.

Another attempt to measure development is the Brandt Line, with which you should be familiar. It was drawn in 1980 to divide the world into rich and poor countries. However, much has changed since it was first drawn and nowadays the Brandt Line is quite out of date.

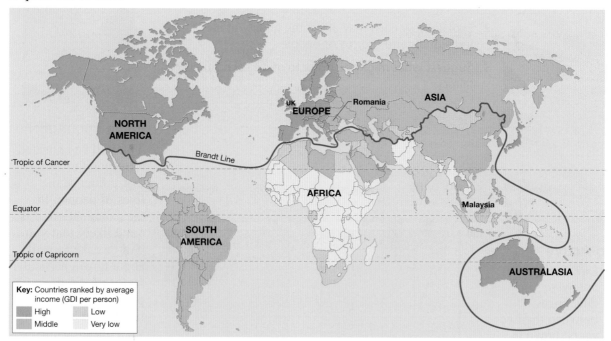

Figure 4 The Brandt Line 25 years on

(a) Which two continents have the greatest proportion of countries with a very low income? [1]
(b) Describe the distribution of countries which have a very low income. [3]
(c) To what extent is the Brandt Line now a useful means of dividing rich and poor countries? [5]

Inside Information

In part (c), you are asked 'To what extent …'. In a question like this you will be expected to look at both the positive and negative aspects before coming to an overall conclusion. In this case, give evidence that it is useful, evidence that it is not and then state which evidence is most convincing.

Development can be defined and measured in many ways. One way is to look at the wealth of a country. However, wealth is not usually shared equally so even a wealthy country can have a lot of poeple living in poverty. Therefore, another way to measure development is to examine the standard of education, health care or political freedom enjoyed by ordinary people. These are usually called measures of social development.

While the Brandt Line only intended to divide the richer and poorer countries of the world, the countries to the north fell into two further groups. The communist countries of eastern Europe and Asia developed at a much slower rate than the capitalist countries of western Europe and North America. Romania is a former communist country, for example, while the UK is classed as part of the capitalist group. When the communist bloc collapsed in the early 1990s, Romania was far behind the economic development of the UK.

In recent years, many of the poorer countries to the south of the Brandt Line have begun to industrialise rapidly. Farming has become mechanised and more people have migrated to the cities to seek work in the growing secondary and tertiary industries. These are known as Newly Industrialised Countries (NICs). Malaysia is one of these.

Indicator	UK	Romania	Malaysia
% urban access to sanitation	100	89	95
% literate over 15 years of age	99	97	89
% of roads that are paved	100	50	80
Life expectancy at birth	79	73	74

Figure 5a Key development indicators

Year	UK	Romania	Malaysia
2000	27	4	21
2005	65	17	49
2006	65	21	52
2007	72	24	56

Figure 5b It's an increasingly smaller world: internet users as a percentage of total population

Go Active

1 Look at the information in Figure 5a. Decide which you think are the least and most important indicators of development. Why do you think this?

2 Which other indicators could *you* have chosen? Why?

3 Google the 'Human Development Report' or 'UNDATA country figures' to find evidence for the indicators *you* have chosen.

4 To what extent does the information you now have support *your* views about the Brandt Line still being useful?

The global village

The term 'global village' was first used in the 1960s to describe how electronic communication, like the telephone, was making worldwide communication easier. It is now more broadly used to reflect the interdependence of countries through the ease of, for example, trade, travel, migrations, the internet and cultural links.

The term globalisation refers to the way individual people and countries are connected to each other at a global scale.

EXAM SPOTLIGHT

Study Figure 5b.
(a) Give one way in which the trend in internet use is similar in the UK and Malaysia. [1]
(b) Compare internet use in Romania with that of Malaysia. [2]
(c) Explain how internet use could help a country develop economically. [2]
(d) Suggest and explain two ways in which internet use might help improve quality of life for people around the world. [4]

What are the advantages and disadvantages of an interdependent world?

Countries depend on each other in many ways: people travel from country to country for work and leisure, goods and services are traded between them and they help each other in the form of aid. A major event in one part of the world is likely to have effects in many other places. Some effects of interdependence are positive while others are negative.

In recent years the collapse of a number of banks in the USA quickly affected the money markets in other countries, causing difficulty for borrowers. In the UK, as with other countries, this prevented people buying houses, persuaded them not to buy new goods such as cars and resulted in higher levels of unemployment. This is known as a depression.

What happens in a depression?

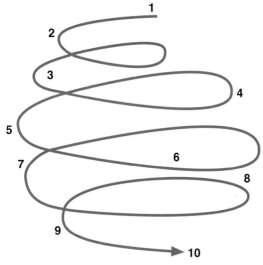

1 Bank loans not repaid
2 Banks lend less money
3 People buy fewer goods
4 Manufacturers make staff redundant
5 Manufacturers' suppliers make staff redundant
6 Less money spent in country
7 Service industries close, lay off staff
8 Less taxes paid
9 Less money for public services
10 Public services reduced, staff made redundant

Figure 6 The negative multiplier

Go Active

For either a Case Study you have worked on in class or an example from your local area, outline the effects of the negative multiplier. Do this by following these steps:

1 Make a copy of the negative multiplier diagram, leaving out the statements.

2 Add statements of your own to include specific places, jobs and numbers of people affected.

Inside Information

You will obviously be given the opportunity to use some of your Case Studies in either exam paper. You may also be able to use some of the information as evidence for the decision you make on the problem solving paper.

However, wherever you use this information, you must give specific detail to gain the highest marks. For example, in this case:

- name actual places
- quote precise figures
- give detail of jobs lost.

The only way you will be able to do this is to revise effectively and practise selecting the right information at the right time.

Positive aspects of interdependence

You have just worked on one example of how interdependence can create problems. Perhaps you can think of others. There are, however, many positive effects.

Go Active

1 Complete a copy of the table below to show how your life is dependent on other parts of the world. Add more rows to display other things that influence you, such as restaurants, holidays and TV programmes.

Article	Country
Article of clothing 1	
Article of clothing 2	
Hot drink	
Canned food	
Fresh fruit	
Electrical equipment	

2 How might your life change if there was not an exchange of goods and services between countries?

3 It is not only you who is affected by this aspect of interdependence. Suggest some advantages for the countries providing you with these goods and services.

It's not always quite so simple!

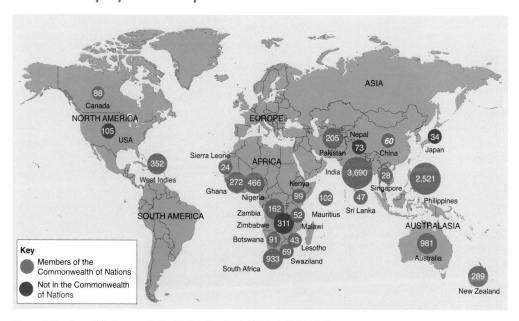

Figure 7 Newly qualified nurses in the NHS trained outside the UK: 2004–5

EXAM SPOTLIGHT

(a) Describe the distribution in the origin countries of nurses. [3]

(b) Complete each of the following sentences to help explain why the nurses migrated to the UK after training. [2]
Most are economically poor countries so …
Most are members of the Commonwealth of Nations so …

(c) On balance, is this migration good or bad? You must refer to effects both in the country of origin, and the destination, in your answer. Look at page 207 of the Student's Book to help you. [5]

How does trade operate?

As we saw on the previous pages, much of the interdependence between countries is the result of trade. Some countries provide certain goods and services while others provide different ones. Traditionally, the UK has depended on the countries of the Commonwealth of Nations (formerly the British Commonwealth) for its primary materials. In turn, it supplied these nations with manufactured goods and services such as banking.

However, trade is now a great deal more complex than that.

There are two basic types of trading agreement:

1 *Free trade*: this involves importing and exporting goods and services without any restrictions.

2 *Restricted trade*: this usually involves protecting a country's own industry by blocking imports from other countries. They may do this by means of quotas, import duty or subsidies.

Quota: A limit placed on the quantity of goods that a country may export to another.	**Import duty**: A tax or tariff that must be paid by a company when goods are exported/imported between countries.	**Subsidy**: A payment made by a country to its own producers, in order to make them more competitive with imported goods.

Member

Candidate

Quotas imposed on many outside goods

Freedom of travel within member countries

Import duties imposed on many outside goods

No import duties on goods produced in member countries

Subsidies for some goods produced in member countries

Freedom to work in member countries

Figure 8 The European Union (EU) – much more than a trading bloc

Go Active

1 Look at the map of EU member countries. List the trade advantages of being a member country of the EU. For each factor you have listed, write a sentence explaining the advantage for a firm manufacturing in the UK.

2 There are some advantages that apply to individuals living in EU countries. Use these advantages to explain how living in an EU country could be beneficial to you in the future.

Free trade – the law of supply and demand

Ghana produces cocoa. Cocoa is made into chocolate. People in the EU eat a great deal of chocolate. Thus, 75 per cent of Ghana's cocoa is exported to EU countries. EU chocolate companies buy the cocoa for the lowest price they can pay. The average income of a cocoa farmer is only about £160 a year.

A surplus of cocoa means there is more cocoa than required, so the price paid to Ghana's farmers goes down. A cocoa deficit means there isn't enough cocoa to meet demand, so the price goes up.

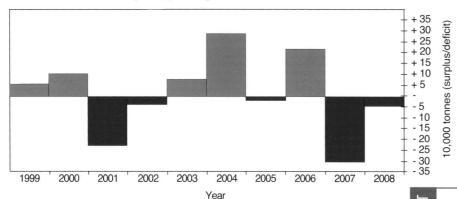

Figure 9 Changes in cocoa supply against demand

Fair trade – for a more equal world

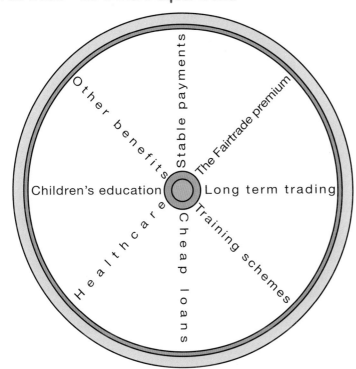

Figure 10 Features of fair trade

(a) Describe the pattern of cocoa deficit and surplus. Use figures in your answer. [3]

(b) 2004 is likely to be the worst year for a cocoa farmer. Explain why. [2]

(c) Which is likely to be the best year for the farmer? Explain your choice. [2]

(b) Suggest and explain two ways in which the pattern you have described is likely to affect the farmer's quality of life. [4]

Case Study – the Knowledge

Use the spokes of the wheel in Figure 10 to help you build up a Case Study Fact file on a Fairtrade project you have either studied in class or can find on the internet.

1 Start by locating the project using a sketch map. Then describe the activities of people involved.

2 Complete the fact file by working your way around the wheel from the top, in a clockwise direction, providing as much detail as you can.

What is the role of aid?

It is not always possible for countries to respond to events that affect them without the help of others. In these situations, help is given in the form of aid. The money and other resources come from three main sources.

Types of aid

Multilateral aid: given by many governments to large international organisations who decide how the aid should be distributed.

Bilateral aid: given by the government of one country to the government of another.

Non-government aid: given by independent organisations, often charities, who collect donations for countries and groups that need help.

Using the aid

Aid may be used for two broad purposes:

1 As a short term measure to help people in an emergency.

2 As a long term measure, in the form of development aid, to help people take control of their lives.

Emergency aid

Congo: Oxfam scales up emergency aid
16th July, 2009

With a surge in rape, forced labour, reprisal attacks and torture in eastern Congo, Oxfam is working to bring clean water and sanitation to those fleeing the violence, reports Coco McCabe.

Desperate: that's the word Oxfam is using to describe the humanitarian situation facing many of the 800,000 people the United Nations says have been forced from their homes in the eastern provinces of the Democratic Republic of Congo since the start of 2009. That's when the Congolese military began a UN-backed offensive against a Rwandan rebel group known as FDLR, or the Forces Démocratique de Libération du Rwanda.

Many of the displaced people are now sheltering with host families, often crowded into single-room houses with poor access to clean water and sanitation. To help meet their needs, Oxfam has set up a rapid response office in Bukavu, a city in the province of South Kivu, and is scaling up its work in North Kivu.

Women and children at Mugunga camp, Goma, North Kivu province, fleeing violence from armed factions in their villages in the northern part of the province. [Photo: Caroline Irby]

Together with a local organisation, Oxfam is now trucking 200,000 litres of clean water each day into major population centres, such as Lubero in North Kivu, where many displaced people have sought refuge. It is also working to rehabilitate the water systems in those communities and is distributing essential household items such as soap and buckets.

Though Oxfam is now helping 130,000 additional people, insecurity is making the delivery of this life-saving aid difficult in some areas. Fighters have cut off the roads to places such as Walikale in North Kivu and also to parts of South Kivu. Oxfam is calling on all parties to the conflict to respect their obligations under international humanitarian law and let aid through.

Colo McCabe, Oxfam GB, 2009

Figure 11 Emergency aid

Case Study – the knowledge

Emergency aid is most often given following a natural disaster like a flood, drought or earthquake. This is not always the case and some emergencies requiring aid are the result of conflict between different groups of people. Use Figure 11 and an atlas to help you answer the following case study question:

- Name an area affected by a disaster.
- Describe its main effects on people.
- Explain the effectiveness of the emergency aid provided.
- You may wish to use information in your own notes to attempt this question.

Development aid – which route should be taken to sustainability?

There is no simple answer to this. In poorer countries, the choice is between using the aid to invest in large scale development projects, such as multi-purpose dams, or a large number of small scale, intermediate technology projects. These can include introducing communications technology to individual villages and the provision of reliable village water supplies. We have already examined these water alternatives on pages 52 and 53 of this book.

The two examples below show aid from the Canadian International Development Agency (CIDA) to countries in Africa. Both were started in the early 1970s.

Location: Mali

Aims:
- to improve village access to basic services
- to provide high quality basic education, especially for girls
- to improve healthcare provision in the villages
- to provide more work opportunities
- to enable the provision of fair loans to farmers.

Some effects:
- Faso Jigi: an organisation of 5000 members in 134 cooperatives. Provides loans and guarantees a fair price and stable income to farmers.
- Sebenikoro Community School: 512 pupils aged 5–12 of which 320 are girls. All teachers are male.
- National Health Sciences Training Institute: improves effectiveness of nurses, paramedics etc.

Location: Tanzania

Aims:
- to set up large scale wheat growing on traditional grazing land
- to export 50 per cent of the wheat and use the rest in a Canadian-operated bakery in Tanzania
- to use machinery imported from Canada
- to provide aid to Tanzania in return for trade with Canada.

Some effects:
- Displacement of the Barabaig pastoral nomad tribe from their traditional lands.
- Provides a source of bread consumed mainly by the urban rich.
- Biosciences Eastern and Central Africa (BECA): helps poor farmers improve their use of farming technology.

EXAM SPOTLIGHT

You will be asked in some parts of the course to express your own opinions. This happens, for example, in the Controlled Assessment item called 'The Issue' as well as on your problem solving paper.

To give you some practice at this, look at the following quotation and then attempt the task:

' … if you ask a Malian farmer what he needs, he will tell you he needs a plough, a pair of oxen and water to irrigate his field. He will not tell you that he needs genetically-modified seed.' Ibrahima Coulibaly, Malian farmer.

- Which of the two aid programmes above best meets Ibrahima Coulibaly's statement about the needs of a farmer? Explain your choice.
- Is your view similar or different to that of Ibrahima? Use detailed information to help you explain why.

Location, location, location

The reasons why an industry locates itself where it does are sometimes very simple but most of the time the decision-making process is quite complex. At a basic level it may be that, for example, an important mineral resource is found in a certain place and therefore must be extracted from there.

On other occasions, all or some of the following factors are taken into account:
- availability of a suitable *site* for development
- the suitability of its *situation*
- transport links
- availability of a suitable workforce
- local or national government incentives.

Let's look at the site and situation first:

Site: The land on which the industrial unit is to be built. Factors like size, flatness, whether it has been built on before (brownfield) or is being built on for the first time (greenfield), may be considered important.

Situation: The land surrounding the site. How is the site located in relation to, for example, transport links, available labour or amenities and pleasant surroundings for the work force.

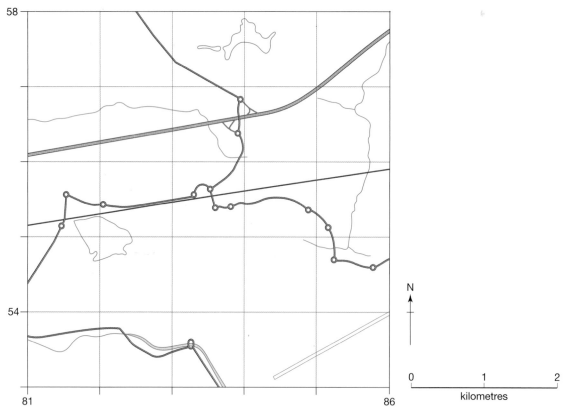

Figure 12 The site and situation of an industrial unit

Case Study – the Knowledge

There are times when it is possible to complete the whole of a Case Study by using a sketch map. No need for any extended writing at all!

You will need a copy of the sketch map on the left and will also need to use the OS map extract on the inside front cover of this book.

Follow this sequence:

1 Label your map to show:
- an M3 motorway junction
- Farnborough Airfield.

2 Shade and label:
- a large built up area
- an area of lake and woodland
- a greenfield area next to the unit.

Add this information to a key. Note that you have not been asked to label the railway line. There is no station in the area covered by the map, so it seems unlikely that it is important to the company.

3 Annotate each of your labels to show their importance to the company. Use the annotations below. One has been elaborated for you. Your annotations should all contain an elaborated 'so what?' statement:
- allows access by air for executives *so* saving them travel time and effort.
- provides a nearby source of labour *so* …
- allows easy access for workers and materials *so* …
- has nearby recreation areas *so* …
- is an area of flat land for future expansion *so* …

By adding a statement that this is the Nokia Research and Development unit at Farnborough in Hampshire, southern England, your completed map has provided a full answer to the following Case Study:

'For a named place of work, describe its situation and explain how its situation benefits the company and its workers.'

Are there Case Studies of your own which you could develop into suitable annotated map responses?

Inside Information

Sometimes you may be *expected* to answer a Case Study using sketch maps but, even if you are not asked to do so, your examiners are likely to be impressed by the use of a sketch map that is well chosen and well drawn.

Can you provide a similar 'sketch map' answer to the Case Study question below?

For a place where access to services has changed:
- Name and locate the place.
- Describe ways in which access to services has changed.
- Explain how the changed access to services has affected different groups of people.

Multinational companies

Rich companies and poor countries

One of the main influences on globalisation are multinational companies (MNCs). These are large companies that have their head office in one city and other offices and factories around the world.

The profits made by the largest MNCs are many times greater than the GNIs of the world's poorest countries. In 2008 the profits of Royal Dutch Shell, an MNC, were US$458 billion. The GNI of the Congo Republic was $15.6 billion. Large MNCs are both rich and powerful.

Figure 13 Cities having the largest number of MNC head offices

Country	GNI per capita (US$)
Burundi	140
Democratic Republic of the Congo	150
Liberia	170
Guinea-Bissau	250
Ethiopia	280
Malawi	290
Eritrea	300
Sierra Leone	320
Niger	330
Mozambique	370

Ten poorest countries: 2008 (source: www.unicef.org)

EXAM SPOTLIGHT

Attempt the following question:
(a) Show the information in the table on a copy of the map in Figure 13.
(b) Describe the distribution of the cities having the largest number of MNC head offices. Use figures in your answer. [3]
(c) Compare this with the distribution of the world's poorest countries. [2]
(d) Suggest reasons for the differences you have described. [4]

Inside Information

By now you should be familiar with this simple checklist to help answer the above question:

(a) You are asked to describe a pattern – don't just list the cities. Refer to continents and hemispheres.

(b) 'Compare' asks you to look for differences and/or similarities. In this example you are likely to be mainly describing differences. Use a word like 'whereas' to help you. Don't be tempted to explain anything here.

(c) This is your opportunity to explain. The question doesn't say how many different points you must make, so you must make that decision. You could make one simple point backed up by at least three 'so what?' statements or go to the other extreme of giving four simple points. You may also give two elaborated points … or one simple point with another having at least a couple of 'so whats?'!

Got the idea?

Multinational companies – why locate there?

UK = 2 ■
Germany = 6 ■

●Munich

Key:
■ Car production factories
▲ Car assembly factories
● Head office

Figure 14 Location of BMW car factories

BMW is one of the world's leading car manufacturing companies. It has its head office in southern Germany and other car production and assembly factories at various locations around the world. The difference between car production and car assembly factories is that the former makes cars from start to finish, whereas the latter assembles cars using parts made elsewhere.

EXAM SPOTLIGHT

Study Figures 13 and 14:
(a) Describe the relationship between BMW factories and the GDP of the world's countries.   [3]
(b) Explain this relationship in terms of:
   (i) potential markets
   (ii) suitable workforce. [4]

Go Active

Complete a copy of the following table to help explain some of the influences on the locations of BMW's factories:

1 Add another factor to the first column.

2 When asked for a factory location, either give a city name or name a country with the help of an atlas.

3 It is likely that you have studied a different example of an MNC. If so, complete the table for that company.

Factor	Explanation	Location of factory
Goods made in EU member countries may be sold in any other member country without paying import duties.	*So the cost of the car reaching the buyer is lower than those made outside the EU, allowing more profit to be made.*	
UK local and national government offer incentives to companies setting up in the country.		
Most MNCs wish to produce close to their headquarters to take advantage of a common language.		
Manufacturers wish to make their goods close to major distant markets.		
Labour costs are often high in the head office country but much lower in other parts of the world.		

Multinational companies: good or bad?

The good?

As you have already seen, multinational companies bring a great deal of investment to an area. This results in *direct employment* – jobs for local people in factories. It also often creates even more direct employment through jobs in associated industries. A car assembly factory, for example, is likely to attract component manufacturers to the area.

Benefits do not end there. You saw the effects of the negative multiplier on page 64 of this book. Investment in an MNC is likely to bring a positive multiplier to the area surrounding the factory and sometimes the country as a whole.

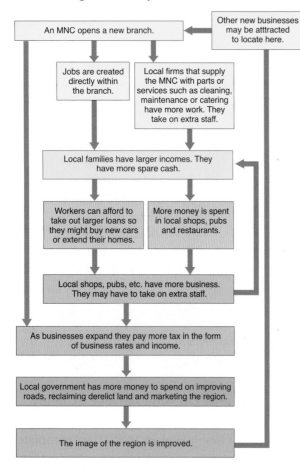

Figure 15 The positive multiplier in action

Go Active

Figure 15 is a basic one. It looks at a process in general terms but does not include any specific detail about the effects of a named MNC setting up a new factory or office somewhere else in the world.

Using information for an MNC you have studied, make a copy of Figure 15 but replace the generic statements with those specific to the MNC you have studied:

- Name the MNC and the place where the new factory or office was set up.
- Name new firms that have opened and the numbers of workers they employ.
- Give detail of local services that have benefited and what the benefits were.
- Describe the changes that have been made to the local area.
- Explain why these may attract more business to the area.

The bad?

Some people argue that multinational companies are not as good for an area as previously may have been suggested. The long term record of some are not especially beneficial and it is possible that the initial positive multiplier may turn negative with time.

Sony sheds 650 jobs with closure

The electronics giant Sony is to close its south Wales manufacturing plant with the loss of 650 jobs because of falling sales of traditional-style TVs. A total of 400 will go at its main factory in Bridgend, by March 2006. Another 250 will be lost at the Pencoed assembly plant, leaving 300 jobs.
The Japanese firm blamed the growth in demand for flat-screen televisions.

Source: BBC News Online: 29 June 2005

Figure 16 The Sony factory opened in Bridgend in 1973

1 Interfere in democratic elections

2 Answer only to their shareholders

3 Have a poor human rights record

4 Cause much environmental damage

Figure 17 Why might it all go wrong?

A sustainable future?

In recent years a great deal of pressure has been placed on MNCs by some national governments, international NGOs and not least by the activities of consumers. As a result of this, principles are devised which state that relations between the MNC and the countries in which it operates should strive toward a more sustainable future for both parties.

WRAP is an independent, US-based organisation that certifies producers in the garment industry – an industry notorious for its performance in many poorer countries and one which supplies many well known MNCs.

What WRAP demands

1 Compliance with local laws and workplace regulations.

2 Prohibition of forced labour.

3 Prohibition of child labour under fourteen years of age.

4 Prohibition of harassment or abuse and corporal punishment.

5 Compensation and benefits at least equal to the legal minimum of the country.

6 Working hours to comply with legal minimum, including at least one day off a week.

7 Prohibition of discrimination for any other reason than ability to do the job.

8 Health and safety at work and in factory-supplied housing.

9 Freedom of association and collective bargaining.

10 Environmentally conscious production.

11 Customs compliance to ensure no illegal shipments of goods.

12 Security to ensure no shipment of, for example, drugs or explosives.

Figure 18 WRAP: Worldwide Responsible Accredited Production

Go Active

It's your turn to decide. MNCs – good or bad?

1 List the positive and negative aspects of MNCs.

2 In your opinion, are they a good or bad influence on the world?

What are the causes and effects of climate change?

Causes

Natural change

Climate change is certainly nothing new. In the past two million years, western Europe has experienced four major Ice Ages. Fossil evidence suggests that between these were periods when temperatures in southern England were tropical.

People

Many scientists believe that the heating Earth is currently experiencing is more rapid than previously experienced. This may be due to the activities of people that have developed, particularly over the past two or three centuries.

Effects

As the world heats up, patterns of air movement will change. It is not simply a matter of everywhere getting hotter. The changes in world climate could seriously affect ecosystems and have major social and economic effects on different groups of people.

Go Active

1 Use information from Figure 19 to write a paragraph explaining how the greenhouse effect works.

2 Use captions A, B and C to help exlain why some scientists believe that people's activities are enhancing the greenhouse effect?

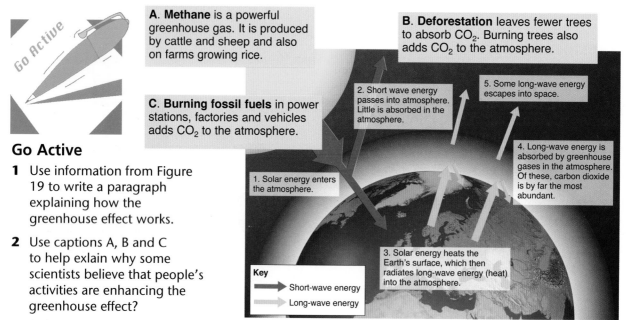

A. **Methane** is a powerful greenhouse gas. It is produced by cattle and sheep and also on farms growing rice.

B. **Deforestation** leaves fewer trees to absorb CO_2. Burning trees also adds CO_2 to the atmosphere.

C. **Burning fossil fuels** in power stations, factories and vehicles adds CO_2 to the atmosphere.

2. Short wave energy passes into atmosphere. Little is absorbed in the atmosphere.

5. Some long-wave energy escapes into space.

1. Solar energy enters the atmosphere.

4. Long-wave energy is absorbed by greenhouse gases in the atmosphere. Of these, carbon dioxide is by far the most abundant.

3. Solar energy heats the Earth's surface, which then radiates long-wave energy (heat) into the atmosphere.

Key
→ Short-wave energy
→ Long-wave energy

Figure 19 The greenhouse effect

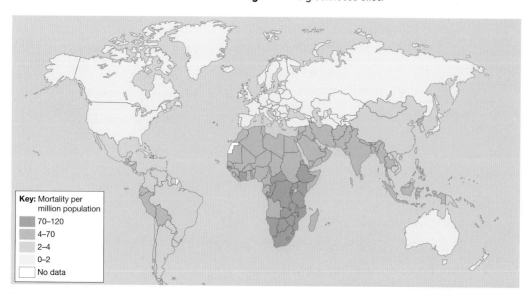

Key: Mortality per million population
70–120
4–70
2–4
0–2
No data

Figure 20 Estimated deaths attributed to climate change in the year 2000, by subregion

Go Active

1 Do a little research using either the internet, school textbooks or your own notes. Label a copy of Figure 20 to show the main effects of global warming on each of the world's continents.

2 Add at least two labels to each continent – don't forget Antarctica! Use information from Figure 21, below, to help.

3 Colour code your labels to show social, economic and environmental effects.

EXAM SPOTLIGHT

Although some questions found on the Higher and Foundation Tier papers are similar, there may be slight differences between them. Take these two questions, for example:

Higher Tier

Explain how governments and individuals may take action to reduce global warming.

Foundation Tier

Explain how people may take action to reduce global warming.

Notice the greater demand of the Higher Tier question, where you must talk about two separate groups of people to attract the highest marks.

Attempt to answer the question appropriate to you. Use the information on pages 77 and 78 to help.

Our globally warmed future

Just like normal weather forecasting, it is hard to know exactly how climates will change in different parts of the world. It is equally difficult to imagine how such changes may affect people and natural environments.

As northern countries warm, disease-carrying insects migrate north.

Parts of Africa and Europe are expected to suffer more severe drought.

As ocean temperatures rise, there could be more frequent and stronger hurricanes.

If ice caps disappear, there will be fewer white surfaces to reflect heat back into space.

Melting ice caps will make the oceans less salty.

Polar ice caps melting will raise sea levels.

Figure 21 Some effects of the enhanced greenhouse effect

Inside Information

This *Exam Spotlight* question above would be marked using a 'levels of response' mark scheme. You work upwards from Level 1 to Level 3, applying guidelines like those on page 53.

- Use the mark scheme to help you write an answer that targets the highest level.
- Don't forget that you only have a time allowance of one minute for each mark.

What are the causes and effects of ecosystem change?

An ecosystem is a system of links between plants and animals and the habitats in which they live. These habitats include such features as soil and climate. Large ecosystems are called biomes. The map in Figure 22 shows the distribution of one of the world's biomes.

Key:
Tropical rainforest

San Jose,
Costa Rica

Figure 22 The tropical rainforest biome

The tropical rainforest relies on rapid recycling of dead plant material. This is possible in the rainforest climate. Deforestation exposes a fragile soil. This quickly erodes and the chances of forest re-growth are low.

EXAM SPOTLIGHT

Describe the distribution of the world's rainforests.   [3]

Inside Information

When answering this question, remember to:
- name areas. In this case you will need to use an atlas to help.
- be specific. For example, which coast of India has an area of rainforest?
- make general statements and add exceptions. For example, where are areas of rainforest found outside the tropics?

Small subsistence farms

Ranching for beef

Mineral extraction

Logging the wood

Infrastructure development

HEP production

Figure 23 Deforested land in Costa Rica

Go Active

1 Draw a quick sketch of the photograph in Figure 23. Label it to show the following:

rainforest   rough grazing land   paths   road   buildings

2 Approximately what percentage of forest remains in the area of the photo?

3 Land exposed in this way to wind and heavy rain is likely to suffer soil erosion. Connect the processes listed below with their correct effects to show some of the effects of this.

Processes	Effects
Minerals in the soil are leached downwards	so carrying capacity is lowered and floods are more frequent.
Soil particles are washed into rivers	so soil becomes less fertile.
Soil material is deposited on the river bed	so river water is less clear and fish habitats are destroyed.

EXAM SPOTLIGHT

(a) Complete a copy of Figure 24 to show that pythons eat fruit bats. [1]

(b) Give a food chain including three components. [2]

(c) Explain what may happen if monkeys were removed from the food web. [4]

Figure 24 A tropical rainforest food web

Tertiary consumer — Jaguar

Secondary consumer — Python   Vampire bat   Tree frog

Primary consumer — Parrot   Fruit bat   Monkey   Insect

Producer — Orchid   Banana tree   Bamboo   Coconut tree

Inside Information

- In (a) make sure your arrow is pointing towards the consumer.
- In (b) you will need to list, in order, one producer, one primary consumer and one secondary consumer. Link them with arrows.
- In (c) the examiner is looking for a sequence of effects, each a consequence of the previous one. Link them as a series of 'So what?' statements.

How might ecosystems be managed sustainably?

It is clear from the last couple of pages that negative effects emerge when people interfere with ecosystems. These effects may be deliberate, as in the case of rain forest destruction, but they may also be unintentional, as with the continuing desertification of the southern edge of the Sahara Desert. This is partly the result of climate change.

The destruction may be on a large scale, as you have seen already, or as small as the use of a local pond to dump waste.

What do we mean by 'sustainable'?

This is the use of resources and environments in ways that will allow them to continue to be used in the future. That is, not destroying them for short term gain. Sustainable development is not restricted to natural environments. It may equally be applied to urban areas and economic development.

EXAM SPOTLIGHT

Study the map in Figure 25. It shows the Mesoamerican Biological Corridor.
(a) Describe the distribution of existing conservation areas. [3]
(b) Explain how the wildlife corridors will help increase the biodiversity of the conservation areas. [4]

Inside Information

These are two separate questions. You will gain <u>no credit</u> for any explanation you give in part (a) because you are only being asked to 'describe'. So, don't use a link word like 'because' until answering part (b).

National Parks: These are set up to protect the forests and ensure that damaging activities are stopped.

Wildlife corridors: These are established by planting trees. This allows migration of animals from area to area of remaining forest.

Medical Reserves: Pharmaceutical companies buy large areas of forest to prevent them being destroyed. They use the forest to find cures for diseases that affect people.

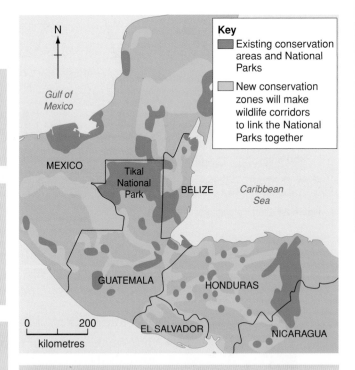

Key
■ Existing conservation areas and National Parks
░ New conservation zones will make wildlife corridors to link the National Parks together

Gulf of Mexico

MEXICO

Tikal National Park

BELIZE

Caribbean Sea

GUATEMALA

HONDURAS

0   200
kilometres

EL SALVADOR

NICARAGUA

Biosphere Reserves: These are similar to National Parks. Increasing amount of human activity is permitted the further away you travel from a central area of unspoiled rainforest. For example:

rainforest ⊠ hunting and collecting allowed ⊠
farming and wood gathering allowed ⊠
settlement allowed ⊠ unprotected forest

Figure 25 Saving the forests?

Sustainable development of an ecosystem: the tropical rainforest

A tropical rainforest is a key ecosystem. Areas of forest absorb carbon dioxide and act as 'lungs of the planet'. Very large forested areas can also affect climate. Thus sensible management of the tropical rainforest ecosystem is crucial.

Go Active

Look back over pages 73 and 74. They show a number of ways in which rainforests are being used. Some of these uses are sustainable, while others are unsustainable.

1 Draw up two lists: one for sustainable uses of the rainforest and the other for unsustainable uses.

2 You may also wish to do this for a different ecosystem you have studied.

Case Study – the Knowledge

Choose one of these Case Study questions to complete:

Foundation Tier

For an ecosystem you have studied:
- Name and locate the ecosystem.
- Describe how it is being used by people.
- Explain how these uses are affecting the environment.

Higher Tier

For an ecosystem you have studied:
- Name and locate the ecosystem.
- Describe how it is being used by people.
- Explain how these uses are affecting both people and the environment.

Go Active

For this rainforest ecosystem or a different ecosystem you have studied, follow this enquiry sequence. Try to find real, named people rather than vague groups.

1 What people feel that there should be *lighter* control over use of the ecosystem? Why do they hold these views?

2 What people feel that there should be *tighter* control over use of the ecosystem? Why do they hold these views?

3 What are your views on the issue? Why do you hold these views?

Inside Information

- Read the question very carefully. You may wish to underline terms asking you to do something or words you consider important.
- You have a limited amount of time for this question. Try not to spend more than 5 or 6 minutes on the Foundation Tier question and 8 or 9 minutes on that for the Higher Tier.
- Mark your finished work using the relevant mark scheme on page 31 of this book.

Manufacturing industry: the environmental price

Different times, different places

The world's first industrial revolution took place in the United Kingdom in the late eighteenth and early nineteenth centuries. For the first time, people were able to mass-produce consumer goods and machinery, in order to help with farming and other activities. People, released from the land, migrated to the cities which were themselves thriving on coalfields, the main source of power.

Since then, many other parts of the world have industrialised. The countries that are industrialising now are known as Newly Industrialised Countries (NICs). China is the largest of these.

Local human effects

Industry leaves behind scarred landscapes in the wake of mineral and coal extraction and old factories often remain derelict in urban areas. Attempts to clear the land may not be wholly successful. In July 2009 for example, people gained compensation following attempts to clear up Corby steelworks after its closure in 1981. The women were exposed to toxic waste and, as a result, their children were born with defects.

Figure 26 Nineteenth-century pollution in Sheffield, UK

Figure 27 Twenty-first century pollution in Beijing, China

Go Active

1. Look at Figures 26 and 27.

2. Make a list of ways in which pollution like this can affect the lives of local people. Add an elaboration ('so what?' statement) to explain each effect.

Wider environmental effects

Whether in the UK or China, the use of fossil fuels as a source of power creates problems that affect natural and built environments, as well as people. They are also likely to have not just local but international effects, such as the environmental damage caused by acid rain.

Figure 28 Acid rain

Go Active

Complete a copy of the following table to show the causes and environmental effects of acid rain. Place the correct number from Figure 28 in the right hand column below.

Statement	Position in Figure 28
Heavy particles drop onto the city, weathering stonework.	
Acid throughflow washes aluminium into rivers and lakes, clogging fish gills and disrupting the breeding of fish and frogs.	
Gases created by burning sulphur, nitrogen and carbon are created in power stations, factories and vehicles.	
Acid rain moves through the soil removing nutrients and adding aluminium. This kills trees and other plants.	
The main gases produced are soluble. They dissolve and travel great distances before falling as acid rain.	
Acid rain and fog damage the leaves of crops, making them stunted and with low yields.	

The enhanced greenhouse effect – a political hot potato

As schools were closing for the 2009 winter holiday, the world's political leaders were leaving Copenhagen having failed to reach a *legally binding* agreement to reduce greenhouse gas emissions at a 'climate change' summit. Earlier in the year, a group of British scientists had been accused of 'hiding' evidence that suggested the activities of people were less important contributors to climate change than most people think.

Below are some views about what might be done that may help explain why it is such a difficult issue.

Richer countries

'We have agreed an 80 per cent cut in greenhouse gas emissions by 2050 so why can't the poorer countries agree to cut by 50 per cent?'

'We will need to monitor the emissions of all countries to make sure they keep within the agreed limits.'

Poorer countries

'Our populations continue to grow and we need to develop our industries. The rich countries have already done this, so why shouldn't we?'

'We don't trust the richer countries. Monitoring emissions will give them the opportunity to gain valuable information about our industries.'

Go Active

The news regarding global warming is constantly changing. Use the internet and radio, TV or newspaper reports to get the latest information.

EXAM SPOTLIGHT

Study the information on the greenhouse effect.
(a) List two reasons why the richer and poorer nations find it difficult to agree how to tackle the issue of global warming. [2]
(b) With which of the two groups do you agree? Explain why you hold these views. [5]

What can we do?

Governments have agreed, in principle, to reduce greenhouse gas emissions but many of the targets look unlikely to be reached. How can individuals help?

Here are ten family strategies to help governments meet their targets:

- Buy local produce.
- Use energy efficient electrical equipment.
- Buy from renewable energy electricity companies.
- Reduce heat loss from the house.
- Buy durable goods.
- Pack the fridge tightly.
- Walk or cycle more often.
- Eat less meat.
- Use public transport.

Go Active

1 Explain how each of the above family strategies will:

- help the government reach its emissions targets
- benefit your family.

2 Have you been counting? Yes, there *are* only nine strategies in the list. Add one of your own and explain its advantages to both your family and the government's attempts to hit its target.

Sustainability: social, economic and environmental

> 'Sustainable development is development that meets the needs of the present without compromising the ability of future generations to meet their own needs.'
>
> Brundtland Report, 1987

Who decides?

Throughout this book there have been brief references to the concept of sustainability. People describe sustainability in different ways. The Brundtland definition above is a commonly accepted one but even this poses more questions than it answers. For example:

- What are the needs at present? Are the 'needs' of a modern society, like private travel and the use of mobile phones, really necessary?
- What are the likely requirements of future generations? How can we tell?

As geographers, we tend to divide sustainability into a number of separate areas:

- Sustainable natural environments. For example, ensuring that rain forests survive in future.
- Sustainable built environments. For example, ensuring that housing and service provisions meet the changing demands of people using them.
- Sustainable economies. For example, ensuring that people of working age are employed and create enough income to meet the future needs of those who do not work.

People rely on the natural environment. It does seem, therefore, that both present and future social and economic needs will only be met if we first meet the needs of the environment.

How sustainable are sustainable activities?

Reusing carrier bags when shopping

Reheating and using yesterday's leftover meal

Boycotting furniture made from tropical hardwoods

Eating only local produce

Taking holidays in the UK

Paying more tax for fuel

Buying a low emission car

Figure 29 Some sustainable options

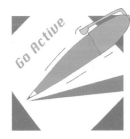

Go Active

1 Look at the statements in Figure 29. Place them along a line, like the one below, according to how sustainable you feel each activity is.

Least sustainable   Most sustainable

2 Add two other strategies to your line:
   - one that is commonly used and which you think is less sustainable than any of the strategies in Figure 29.
   - one that is commonly used and which you think is more sustainable than any of the strategies in Figure 29.

3 Ask a friend or member of your family to attempt the same exercise. Compare and discuss the differences you have.

Problem Solving

A different type of examination

This examination experience is officially part of 'Unit Two'. It will probably be the last GCSE geography examination you take – but possibly not!

You will remember from reading the introduction to this book that you have many options regarding when you take the two examinations.

If you haven't yet read the introduction, it is still worthwhile – in it you will find very important information which will help you get the most out of this book … and your examinations.

Anyway, back to the purpose of this final chapter; problem solving.

Problem solving – a unique experience

The problem solving paper has a number of features. Some of these are identical to those in the other examination you will take, while others are unique to problem solving.

Features of both examinations

1 Resources are used as starting points for each part of the examination. You will be asked to either read or complete a resource, before answering other questions designed to help you show your knowledge and understanding.

2 The examination is stepped. As each new resource is introduced, the level of difficulty is lowered. This is designed to help you work your way through the exam and should boost your confidence. The graph below demonstrates the design of an examination question:

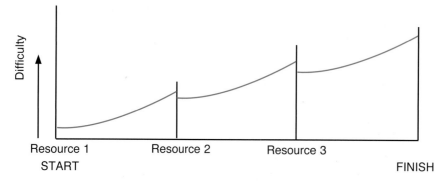

Go Active

'Should a dam be built for a river in Uganda, an east African country?'

This problem solver looks at the following main areas of geography:

- processes of river erosion (physical)
- effects of people's interference with a river (physical)
- need for water and electricity in a poor country (human).

    (a) Complete a similar statement for each of the other two boxed questions on page 81.

    (b) Discuss with a friend the main areas of geography you have decided upon.

Features unique to problem solving

1 Your examiners really want to know how you would solve a geographical problem. This examination paper will take you through a series of questions, finishing with a chance for you to say what you think and to explain why you think it.

Take this opportunity; adults don't ask the opinions of young people like you often enough.

2 The problem solving experience is written to test your knowledge and understanding of an issue that cuts across human and physical geography. Issues that have appeared in the past include:

Should a dam be built for a river in Uganda, an east African country?

Should a part of the Yorkshire coast be protected against erosion?

How should Madagascar's rainforest best be developed in future?

Tackling a problem solving experience

Over the next few pages, you will be taken through the complete problem solving experience. There are two sets of questions, those for the Foundation Tier and those for the Higher Tier. Looking at both sets of questions may be useful in deciding which Tier will be the best for you.

You will probably have experienced many different Foundation and Higher Tier questions in class. If not, it is probably a good idea for you to try and answer both papers before deciding which level of examination you will sit. Do you find the Higher Tier just challenging or very off-putting? Is the Foundation Tier experience supportive or just too simple?

The exam paper that follows looks at a commuter village near Nottingham and the problems it faces due to flooding. It explores the different options available to prevent flooding. It also asks you to decide which method should be used for the future protection of the village.

		Marks	
		Foundation	**Higher**
Part A	This looks at a commuter village near Nottingham and the problems it faces from flooding.	28	25
Part B	This explores the different options available to prevent flooding.	21	21
Part C	This asks you to decide which method should be used for the future protection of the village.	11	14
	Total marks	**60**	**60**

Foundation Tier – Part A

This part looks at a commuter village near Nottingham and the problems it faces from flooding.

You are advised to spend about 30 minutes on this part.

(a) Study Map 1 in the Resource Folder (page 95).

    (i) Complete the following passage by circling the correct answers. [3]

        The river Trent has its source in **Birmingham/Stoke-on-Trent/ the Peak District**. Between Stoke and Nottingham it is joined by several tributaries, including the rivers Dove, Derwent and **Humber/Leicester/Soar**. After Nottingham, it flows mainly **south/ north/west** towards the North Sea.

    (ii) What is meant by the 'estuary' of a river? [1]

        An estuary is _____

    (iii) Complete the following passage to describe the location of the village of Attenborough. [2]

        Attenborough is found _____ kilometres in a

        _____ direction from Nottingham.

(b) Study the OS map extract on the inside back cover. It shows the village of Attenborough. Attenborough is a commuter settlement for Nottingham.

    (i) What is a commuter settlement? [1]

    _____

    (ii) Use map evidence to suggest and explain two reasons why Attenborough is a commuter settlement. [4]

        Reason 1: _____

        Explanation: _____

        _____

        Reason 2: _____

        Explanation: _____

        _____

(c) **(i)** Complete the flood hydrograph below using the following figures. [2]

        On Day 10 rainfall was 10 mm.

        On Day 10 discharge was 500 cumecs.

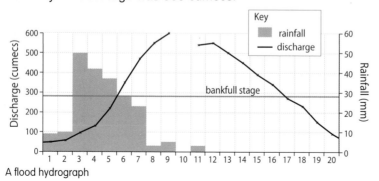

A flood hydrograph

(ii) Use information from the hydrograph to complete the passage below. Choose words from the box. [3]

'Peak discharge came _____ days after peak rainfall. The period when the river was in flood lasted a total of _____ days. The rise of discharge was more than its fall.'

| six | steep | seven | shallow | eleven | even |

(iii) Complete the following causes and effects to help explain why flooding takes place. One has been done for you. [3]

spring snow melt   water goes quickly to river through drains

a high water table   adds to water coming from rainfall

chopping down forests   less infiltration and more surface runoff

more urban areas   less transpiration and interception

(d) Study the passage below. It was written by someone whose house was flooded in Attenborough in November 2000.

'The house was quiet – no TV that night – and we worked quickly to try and move belongings upstairs. The TV went on the table in the kitchen – better lose the table than the telly! Records, CDs, photos and irreplaceable stuff was taken upstairs and piles of leftover blockpaving bricks were put in carrier bags onto which the furniture could be raised. It seems futile now that we put the blocks in bags but we felt they'd spoil the carpets otherwise!'

(i) List two ways in which people tried to save their belongings. [2]

First way: _____

Second way: _____

(ii) Explain the effects of flooding on the quality of life of the people who live in the house. [3]

(iii) Suggest and explain one effect of the November 2000 floods on the natural environment and one effect on transport in the area. [4]

Effect on the natural environment _____

Explanation _____

Effect on transport _____

Explanation _____

[Total mark: 28]

Inside Information

- Remember, the period of flood is when the discharge is above bankfull stage.

Inside Information

- It's perhaps better to do this one in pencil, otherwise it could be very messy if you made a mistake and wanted to change your mind!

Inside Information

- There is no need to do anything more than give information from the passage.

Inside Information

- Think about the area you studied in class and the effects of that flood.
- Use that information and the OS map to help you answer the question.

Part B

This part explores different options available to prevent flooding.

You are advised to spend about 25 minutes on this part.

(a) Study the OS map extract on the inside back cover.

    (i) Give two features of flood defence Option 1. [2]

    First feature: _____

    _____

    Second feature: _____

    _____

    (ii) Give one way in which Option 2 differs from Option 1. [1]

    _____

    (iii) Suggest one advantage and one disadvantage of Option 1 for people living at grid reference 520343. Explain how each will affect the lives of the people. [4]

    Advantage: _____

    _____

    Effect on lives of people: _____

    _____

    Disadvantage: _____

    _____

    Effect on lives of people:_____

(b) Study Photograph 1 in the Resource Folder (page 95) and the OS map extract on the inside back cover.

    (i) Give a four-figure grid reference for Attenborough Cricket Club. [1]

    Grid reference: _____

    (ii) Suggest why Attenborough Cricket Club members may prefer flood defence Option 2. [2]

    _____

    _____

    _____

    (iii) Name a group of people who may disagree with Option 2. Explain why they may disagree with this option. [4]

    Name of group: _____

    Why they may disagree with Option 2: _____

    _____

    _____

    _____

    _____

Inside Information

- The use of grid references and named features will help you earn full marks.

Inside Information

- Each advantage should be a simple statement and the effect on people a 'so what?' statement.

Inside Information

- Think about another activity that may take place along the river and be disrupted by the building of a wall.

(c) Study Photograph 2 in the Resource Folder (page 96).

    (i) Describe how Carsington Water is used for water storage.   [1]

_____

_____

    (ii) Explain how Carsington Water may help to prevent flooding along the River Trent.   [2]

_____

_____

_____

Inside Information

- What do the captions around the photos tell you?

    (iii) Use photograph evidence to explain how Carsington Water may help improve the quality of life of people living in nearby urban areas.   [4]

_____

_____

_____

_____

_____

_____

[Total mark: 21]

Inside Information

- This question will be marked using a levels scheme like that on page 59.
- You must quote specific evidence from the photograph to gain high marks.

Part C

This part asks you to decide which method should be used for the future protection of the village.

You are advised to spend about 35 minutes on this part.

You are asked to advise which of the three flood defence options should be developed for the protection of Attenborough: **Local Option 1**, **Local Option 2 or a new reservoir in the catchment area**.

Use the Fact file in the Resource Folder (page 96) to complete the following matrix, which will help you organise your ideas. Some of the table has been completed for you.

You should spend about 15 minutes completing the matrix.

Use the information in the matrix on page 86 to help you write a letter explaining how you would protect Attenborough from flooding. You may also use information from other parts of this paper and ideas of your own.

You should advise which one option should be developed.

Explain why your choice is better than the other *two* options.

I am writing to advise the development of **Local Option 1**, **Local Option 2, a new reservoir**. (Circle your chosen economic activity.)

I have chosen this because _____

_____

_____

_____

Inside Information

- You will be given roughly a page and a half of lined paper on which to write your letter. You should certainly need no more space than that and, probably, a little less.

Option	Fact	Supports (S) or rejects (R) the option and why
Local Option 1	Will have a wall that will be landscaped to look natural	(S) It will still look pleasing to local people, so they will be happy to continue living there.
Local Option 2		
A new reservoir		

Completing the matrix
- The matrix is very important to your success in problem solving.
- Its main purpose is to help you organise some ideas, so that you are able to write a letter explaining what you think should happen and why you think this.

A useful backstop
- While you can only get the highest marks for a carefully thought out letter, the matrix could also be worth valuable marks.
- If you fail to score more than 8 out of the 11 marks available for this part of the paper, your examiner will go back and mark the matrix.

What is it worth?
- A perfectly completed matrix, showing clear geographical understanding in the right hand column, will be awarded 8 marks.

The message
- Make sure you complete the matrix to the best of your ability.
- Include elaborated 'so what?' statements in the right hand column. Even if you don't end up with a brilliant letter, this may still earn you over two thirds of the available marks.

Inside Information

How do I tackle this section?

- Decide which of the three strategies you think is best. Don't forget to circle it.
- Now work out a structure for your letter.
  For example, if you decide to choose Local Option 1 your plan will be something like this:

I have chosen this option because it offers more advantages than the other two.

Local Option 2 has some advantages. These are ...

However its disadvantages outweigh the advantages. These are ...

Similarly, building a new reservoir has advantages. These include ...

However, the disadvantages of a new reservoir are more convincing. These include ...

Therefore, my choice of Local Option 1 is better than the other two, although it does have the following disadvantages ...

The advantages are great. These are ...

So, to sum up, Local Option 1 is better on balance than the other strategies available.

To get the highest marks you will need to:

- use elaborated 'so what?' statements. Letters that just repeat information from the resources only get marks from the lowest level.
- think about both the effects on people and the environment.
- bring in information from your studies. Perhaps you have already looked in class at flooding and how to control the flood risk. Use this information to back up your arguments.
- consider the short and long term effects of the strategies.
- be concise. Don't go on and on. Use any more than the one and a half sides provided and you are likely to be just repeating things you have already stated.
- write this letter in your best possible English, or Welsh if your paper is in that language. It will be marked for its spelling and grammar.
- use the correct geographical terms.

Higher Tier – Part A

This part looks at a commuter village near Nottingham and the problems it faces from flooding.

You are advised to spend about 25 minutes on this part.

(a) Study Map 1 in the Resource Folder (page 95).

   (i) Describe the course of the River Trent. [3]

   _____

   _____

   _____

   _____

   _____

   (ii) Describe the location of Attenborough. [2]

   _____

   _____

   _____

(b) Study the OS map extract on the inside back cover.

   Use information from this map and Map 1 in the Resource Folder (page 95) to give and explain two reasons why Attenborough is a commuter settlement for Nottingham. [4]

   Reason 1: _____

   _____

   Reason 2: _____

   _____

(c) Study the flood hydrograph below.

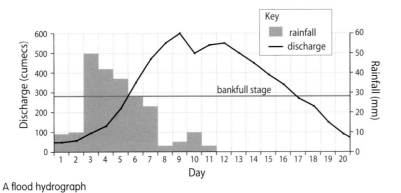

A flood hydrograph

   (i) What is the lag time following peak rainfall? [1]

   _____

   _____

   (ii) For how many days did the river flood? [1]

   _____

Inside Information
- Use geographical terms like 'source' and 'mouth' when describing the river's course.
- Direction and distances would also help.

Inside Information
- An accurate distance and direction from another feature on the map is all that is needed.
- Look at the structure of the equivalent question on the Foundation Tier.

Inside Information
- Each reason requires a simple statement followed by its elaboration (the 'so what?' statement).

Inside Information
- The lag time is the delay between peak rainfall and peak discharge.

Inside Information
- The river is in flood when discharge is above bankfull stage.

(iii) Describe the changes in discharge rate over the entire time period. Use figures in your answer. [3]

_____

_____

_____

_____

_____

(iv) Explain how the activities of people may increase flood risk. [3]

_____

_____

_____

_____

_____

Inside Information

- The examiner is only looking for the activities of people here. Don't give natural causes.

(d) Study the passage below. It was written by someone whose house was flooded in Attenborough in November 2000.

'The house was quiet – no TV that night – and we worked quickly to try and move belongings upstairs. The TV went on the table in the kitchen – better lose the table than the telly! Records, CDs, photos and irreplaceable stuff was taken upstairs and piles of leftover blockpaving bricks were put in carrier bags onto which the furniture could be raised.

We stuffed a few things into a bag or two and climbed awkwardly into the boat – I think it was a boat but they were also using a tractor to evacuate people so it could have been that. Before I left I turned off the gas and electricity and locked the door.'

(i) Explain the effects of flooding on the quality of life of the people who live in the house. [3]

_____

_____

_____

_____

_____

Inside Information

- The key to this question is 'quality of life'.
- You will gain a maximum of one mark for just quoting information from the passage.

(ii) Use evidence from the OS map extract to help you suggest and explain how the November 2000 floods affected the natural environment and transport in the area. [5]

_____

_____

_____

_____

_____

_____

_____

[Total mark: 25]

Inside Information

- This question will be marked using a levels scheme similar to that on page 59 of this book.
- You must write about both the natural environment and transport to stand a chance of gaining full marks.

Part B

This part explores different options to prevent flooding.

You are advised to spend about 25 minutes on this part.

(a) Study the OS map extract on the inside back cover.

    (i) Describe the route taken by flood defence Option 1.   [3]

_____

_____

_____

_____

_____

Inside Information

- The use of grid references and named features will help you earn full marks.

    (ii) Suggest how Option 1 may have both positive and negative effects on people living at grid reference 520343.   [4]

_____

_____

_____

_____

_____

Inside Information

- You will receive a maximum of three marks if you refer to only positive or negative effects.

(b) Study Photograph 1 in the Resource Folder (page 95) and the OS map extract on the inside back cover.

    (i) Describe the location of Attenborough Cricket Club.   [2]

_____

_____

_____

Inside Information

- Use direct map evidence including grid references.

    (ii) Suggest how choosing Option 2 to protect Attenborough from flooding may affect different groups of people.   [4]

_____

_____

_____

_____

_____

_____

Inside Information

- Select groups having contrasting effects – ideally one positive and the other negative.

(c) Study Photograph 2 in the Resource Folder (page 96).

(i) Explain how the use of Carsington Water may help prevent flooding in the Trent valley. [3]

_____

_____

_____

_____

_____

(ii) Use photographic evidence to suggest how Carsington Water may have affected the lives of both local people and visitors from urban areas. [5]

_____

_____

_____

_____

_____

_____

_____

[Total mark: 21]

Inside Information

- Use evidence from the photo captions to help you.
- This question will be marked using a levels scheme like that on page 59.
- Make sure you include specific detail to gain the highest mark.

Part C

This part asks you to decide which method should be used for the future protection and sustainable development of the village.

You are advised to spend about **40 minutes** on this part.

You are asked to advise which of the three flood defence options should be developed for the protection and sustainable development of Attenborough: **Local Option 1, Local Option 2 or more reservoirs in the catchment area**.

Use the fact file in the Resource Folder (page 96) to complete the following matrix to help you organise your ideas. Some of the table has been completed for you.

You should spend about **20 minutes** completing the matrix.

Inside Information

Completing the matrix
- This is a staging post on the way to completing your report.

Main purpose
- To help you organise the new ideas you see in the fact file and add some of your own. These may come from other resources you have seen in the examination and ideas you have brought from your studies in geography. They will aid your writing of the final report.

A useful backstop
- While you can only get the highest marks for a carefully executed report, the matrix could also be worth valuable marks.
- If you fail to score more than 8 of the 14 marks available for this part of the paper, your examiner will go back and mark the matrix.

What is it worth?
- A perfectly completed matrix, showing clear geographical understanding in the two right hand columns, will be awarded 8 marks.
- You will need to be sure you understand all aspects of sustainability if you are to score highly.

The message
- Even if you feel that you are likely to score high marks on the report, it is advisable to complete the matrix. It may just act as a confidence booster and will provide you with some form of framework around which to base the report.
- It is also there to give you practice at providing 'so what?' statements and clarity of thought in relation to sustainability, which will attract the highest marks.

	Fact	Effects	Sustainable (S) Not sustainable (N)
Local Option 1	Landscaped and natural wall	Will maintain the rural 'feel' of the village and be visually appealing to residents.	(S) Will encourage people to continue living in the village so maintaining the local economy.
Local Option 2			
A new reservoir			

Use the information in your matrix on page 93 to help you write a report advising how to protect Attenborough from flooding and promote its sustainable development. You may also use information from other parts of this paper and ideas of your own.

You should advise which **one option** should be developed.

Explain why your choice is better than the other *two* options.

I am writing to advise the development of ...

Insert your choice of strategy from **Local Option 1/Local Option 2/a new reservoir**.

You will be given roughly two pages of lined paper on which to write your letter. You should certainly need no more space than that and, probably, a little less.

Inside Information

Planning – the key to success

- consider the options carefully. Use evidence from not only the fact file but also other resources you have used and your wider understanding to inform your choice.
- now work out a structure for your report. It should include:
  - a clear statement of the chosen strategy
  - a consideration of the advantages and disadvantages of the two rejected strategies, with an emphasis on the disadvantages
  - a consideration of the disadvantages and advantages of your chosen strategy, with an emphasis on the advantages
  - a final statement briefly restating your choice
  - of greatest importance, ideas of sustainability woven throughout your report.

To reach the higher levels of the mark scheme you will need to:

- use the simple statements in the fact file and other evidence as starting points. Investigation of these will need to trigger elaborated thinking aimed at demonstrating your full understanding.
- consider the social, economic and environmental implications of the strategies.
- import your own knowledge if it helps to support the views you are expressing.
- consider the short and long term effects of the strategies. This is a large part of sustainability.
- write your report in a formal style. Get straight to the point and don't be tempted to waffle. You should not need any more space than the approximate two pages provided for your response.
- write this letter in your best possible English, or Welsh if your paper is in that language. It will be marked for its spelling and grammar.
- include relevant geographical terms wherever possible.

Resource Folder

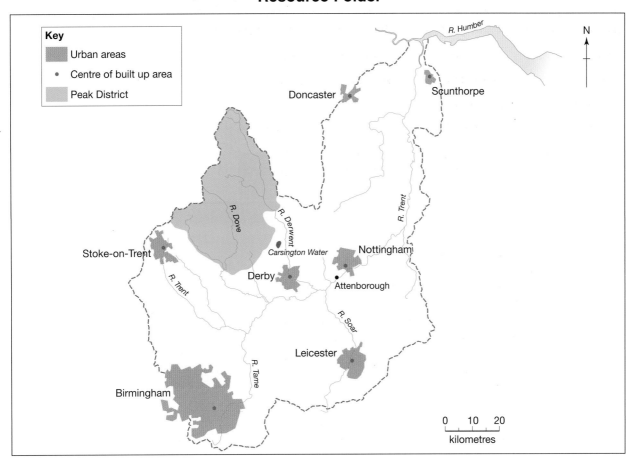

Map 1 The River Trent Drainage Basin

Photograph 1 Attenborough Cricket Club

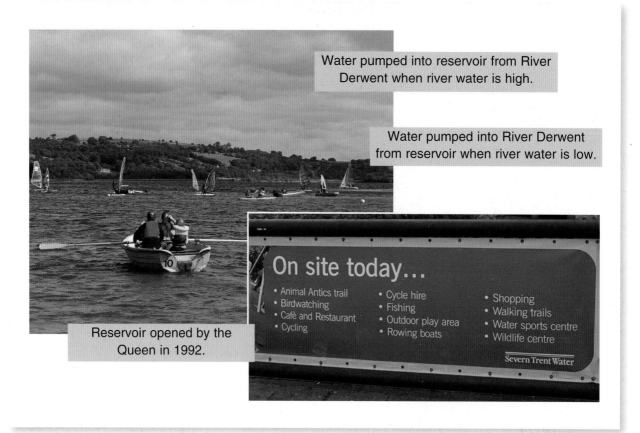

Water pumped into reservoir from River Derwent when river water is high.

Water pumped into River Derwent from reservoir when river water is low.

On site today...
- Animal Antics trail
- Birdwatching
- Cafè and Restaurant
- Cycling
- Cycle hire
- Fishing
- Outdoor play area
- Rowing boats
- Shopping
- Walking trails
- Water sports centre
- Wildlife centre

Severn Trent Water

Reservoir opened by the Queen in 1992.

Photograph 2 Carsington Water

FACT FILE

Local Option 1
- will have a wall that will be landscaped to look natural
- will have flood gates that allow access to car park and sports pavilions
- will destroy 305 metres of ancient hedgerows.

Local Option 2
- will cause some damage to Attenborough Nature Reserve
- will make the river difficult to use by fishers
- will protect recreation land, including the cricket pitch.

A new reservoir
- creates a range of wildlife habitats
- drowns farmland and farm buildings
- provides water for people in Nottingham and Derby.